"Tamara McClintock Greenberg's workbook engages readers in a conversa[tion about the] real-life dilemmas posed by complex post-traumatic stress disorder (C-PTS[D)…] and nuanced ways to harness the power of four 'A's—acceptance, awaren[ess…] truly valuable resource for people recovering from C-PTSD and their therapists."

—**Julian D. Ford, PhD, ABPP**, past president of the International Society for Traumatic Stress Studies, and professor at the University of Connecticut Health Center

"Quite simply the best workbook for clients dealing with trauma. It's both incredibly insightful as well as accessible, with an astute sense of what clients who have lost their identities because of adult and child-hood adversity need. This book provides nurturing and healing advice that will benefit all trauma survivors. Greenberg's deep empathy and compassion is on every page. It also serves as a vital resource for clinicians working with clients who have C-PTSD. In time, this will be a staple of every clinician's library."

—**Dan Hocoy, PhD**, president of Goddard College, licensed clinical psychologist, and coeditor of APA *Handbook of Humanistic and Existential Psychology*

"*The Complex PTSD Coping Skills Workbook* is a wonderful resource for anyone who has ongoing distress as a result of multiple negative or traumatic events. Incorporating clinical experience, research findings, and a deep, compassionate understanding of the issues, Greenberg has created a practical, supportive workbook that can be used alone or with a therapist to find 'a path to feeling and being more in control of your life'."

—**Elizabeth McMahon, PhD**, psychologist, and author of *Overcoming Anxiety and Panic Interactive Guide* and *Virtual Reality Therapy for Anxiety*

"An informative, engaging, and highly practical workbook. Greenberg provides the reader with a range of clearly articulated strategies for dealing with the aftermath of complex trauma: from noticing and accept-ing anger, to managing dissociation, to finding a therapist. The guidance is excellent: firmly rooted in theory, evidence, and the latest clinical wisdom. I highly recommend this book."

—**Mick Cooper**, professor of counseling psychology at the University of Roehampton, London; and coauthor of *Personalizing Psychotherapy*

"*The Complex PTSD Coping Skills Workbook* provides an extraordinarily powerful road map for treating complex trauma. Tamara Greenberg's respectful and inviting tone is sure to make this a classic workbook. All C-PTSD patients, families, and therapists need to get this book."

—**Louann Brizendine, MD**, neuropsychiatrist, and *New York Times* bestselling author of
The Female Brain and *The Upgrade*

"In this workbook, Tamara Greenberg once again gifts us with her masterful blend of theory (defining C-PTSD), clarity of understanding underlying multiple issues such as dissociation and substance abuse, practical lessons for managing difficult emotions and relationships, and finding the right therapist—and finally always with her wise and compassionate voice."

—**Ilene A. Serlin, PhD, BC-DMT**, coeditor of *Integrated Care for the Traumatized*

"Trustfully inviting, this workbook is both intensely personal while universal in its helpful information and deep wisdom. As a physician witnessing women's lives for over forty years, this single volume unlocks areas of confusion and frustration that increasingly have separated people from more joyful living. Greenberg shares stories from her many years as a therapist and guides the reader through an efficient, productive, and self-affirming healing journey."

—**Ricki Pollycove, MD, MS, FACOG, FNCBC**, fellow of the American Congress of
Obstetrics and Gynecology, author of *The Pocket Idiot's Guide to Bioidentical Hormones*, and
coauthor of *Mother Nurture*

"This has been such a wonderful read. This workbook is perfectly timed, and not only defines C-PTSD but reflects on its pernicious effects. Tamara really breaks down the impact of C-PTSD and provides practical tools for navigating through its challenges. This book is a wonderful resource for individuals interested in healing and understanding how to support others suffering from C-PTSD."

—**Ankhesenamun Ball, PsyD**, clinical neuropsychologist; and clinical director of Being,
A Psychological Corporation

"A marvelous workbook! Tamara McClintock Greenberg writes a wonderfully accessible and practical guide for anyone who has experienced trauma, and in particular, for those who are living with C-PTSD. The stories, vignettes, explanations, checklists, and reflective exercises provide an exquisitely constructed, down-to-earth road map for promoting change. This resource destigmatizes C-PTSD and brilliantly leads the reader to take the fear out of facing trauma."

—**Erick Hung, MD**, professor of clinical psychiatry at the University of California, San Francisco

The Complex PTSD Coping Skills Workbook

An Evidence-Based Approach to Manage Fear and Anger, Build Confidence, and Reclaim Your Identity

TAMARA McCLINTOCK GREENBERG, PsyD

New Harbinger Publications, Inc.

Publisher's Note

This publication is designed to provide accurate and authoritative information in regard to the subject matter covered. It is sold with the understanding that the publisher is not engaged in rendering psychological, financial, legal, or other professional services. If expert assistance or counseling is needed, the services of a competent professional should be sought.

NEW HARBINGER PUBLICATIONS is a registered trademark of New Harbinger Publications, Inc.

New Harbinger Publications is an employee-owned company.

Figure 2.1, depicting the HPA Axis, also appeared in *Treating Complex Trauma* by Tamara McClintock Greenberg, copyright © 2020 Tamara McClintock Greenberg/Springer Nature.

The Cooper–Norcross Inventory of Preferences (C–NIP) is copyright © 2015 by Mick Cooper and John Norcross. Used with permission.

Cover design by Amy Daniel

Acquired by Wendy Millstine and Jess O'Brien

Library of Congress Cataloging-in-Publication Data on file

Printed in the United States of America

26   25   24

10   9   8   7   6   5   4

Contents

Introduction

If you've picked up this book, I'll guess you've experienced some difficult things in your life—and that you are also incredibly resilient. This is common in trauma survivors (and one reason we as a culture often focus on the concept of "surviving," not victimhood).

Complex post-traumatic stress disorder, or CPTSD, occurs when you have experienced what's known as complex trauma. This is trauma that's caused not by one discrete traumatic event but by multiple events, usually beginning in childhood, that have profound impacts on your self-concept and your ways of relating to others. CPTSD happens based on the aggregate of trauma; it represents what is often a life filled with difficulties. As such, the symptoms of CPTSD can be more severe, long-lasting and woven into your personality, which is different than what happens with post-traumatic stress disorder (PTSD).

As you'll hear me describe, CPTSD has a profound impact on identity. Early and repeated traumas take away important aspects of our sense of self; ultimately they result in a kind of *identity theft*. They can cause us to be unclear about our true thoughts and feelings and can make us unsure of the kinds of people we want or need to be around. It makes it hard to know how to be assertive; it makes it hard to know how we can take care of ourselves. Who you really are can be confusing, especially if your history is murky and unclear, with limited or disjointed narratives. And when you're in this situation, anger, fear, and uncertainty can become a powerful presence in your life and in ways that are often unwelcome.

This book aims to help you understand your complex trauma and the way it has impacted your entire life and your identity. I'm honored that you are here, and I hope that I can provide tools and ideas to reclaim aspects of your life that may have been stolen because of what you have had to endure.

Complex trauma involves multiple betrayals, including overt abuse, neglect, and having to experience difficult circumstances way before you should have to. It also involves traumas experienced as an adult. These experiences can make it tough to know how to take care of yourself. I will help you with the first part of the standard treatment for CPTSD, which is understanding the *neurobiology of trauma*—what's commonly known as the fight/flight/freeze response—so you can create a basic sense of safety for yourself in your life; learning healthier coping skills for intrusive experiences of fear, anger, and anxiety; building the basics of meta-cognition (or your ability to think about your own thinking); and building social support to help you deal with your CPTSD. We'll also talk about some of the more challenging aspects of CPTSD symptoms, like substance use and suicidal thoughts, and learn coping mechanisms for those painful and frightening experiences. as well as some ideas of when it might be good to ask for help.

The second part of treatment—dealing with the memories of your traumatic experience through cognitive behavioral therapy, exposure therapy, EMDR, psychodynamic therapy, and other techniques—is something a professional can help you with, because it is beyond the scope of this workbook. It's also true that you may not need or want to take this step. Ultimately, it depends on your experience of CPTSD, and what you feel you need once the symptoms of CPTSD that most affect your day-to-day life and your core sense of self have been addressed. That said, an entire chapter in this book is devoted to thinking about how to find a therapist using research that explains, to the best of our knowledge, how healing in therapy works and what kinds of therapists and treatments may be right for you.

How to Use This Book

The really great thing about a workbook is you can use parts of it or all of it, in large chunks or small doses. Take on aspects of this book as it feels right for you. You can use the book alone, or with someone you trust, like a therapist. Do keep in mind that not all aspects of the book may be ones you can relate to; keep your individual journey in mind as you read. Also consider that though some of the skills and ideas in this book may seem simple to absorb, often true change means revisiting some of the same ideas in different moods and states of mind. So, patience and persistence are key. There are also some additional materials at the website for this book, like worksheets and a bonus chapter to educate loved ones about CPTSD symptoms: http://www.newharbinger.com/49708. (See the very back of the book for more details.)

Finally, keep in mind that since this is a book about trauma, there are times when I will discuss material (in composite form, not related to any one person) related to some of the more difficult things people with CPTSD have experienced. I want you to know that it's always a mixed thing to provide case examples in a book like this, and I do so with as little detail as possible while still speaking to you—and to also indicate that I can empathize as best as I can with the kinds of trauma that you may have been subjected to. I do describe emotional, physical, and sexual abuse as well as neglect—again, in as vague detail as possible, but it's there. It can be intense and a lot to read—and if it's too much, please feel free to do what you might in a scary movie—hit fast-forward and skip to the coping skills. However, if the material is consistently triggering or painful, I encourage you to note what you're reacting to and discuss it with your therapist or clinician.

A Note on the COVID-19 Pandemic

I wrote a large part of this book during 2020, one of the more challenging years of my life—and I'm guessing yours too. None of us could have predicted that a global pandemic would upend everything we once took for granted. The disruptions were endless but included limits to our personal freedom, our ability to seek and give comfort in the usual ways. We lost closeness in aspects that are obvious, like not being able to have our loved ones over for dinner and not being able to visit elders in care facilities. But we lost personal connections in small ways, too. We missed chatting with colleagues in our offices, gossiping with neighbors and even the banters with taxi and rideshare drivers. Suddenly, we could not exercise like we did, go to a movie, or eat food in public places without fear. We became more alone, though social media persisted and for some became a main source of contact with the external world. However, social media is a very mixed thing. On the one hand, it reminded us there were others going through what we were. On the other, our internet communities seemed to silently shame us if we were rightfully sad and scared about the unbelievable numbers of deaths instead of harnessing our sourdough bread–baking skills, or learning a new instrument or new language. The pandemic challenged self-concepts for everyone, but even more so for survivors of trauma, who may have a shaky or limited sense of self to begin with.

Yet, I noticed something remarkable among many of my clients with CPTSD. Locked down with fewer distractions, many people took the opportunity to try to understand themselves, their lives, and their relationships better. Of course, this was not simply because of opportunity; the lack of diversions led to increases in symptoms among many people—flashbacks, nightmares, increases in fear and anger related to the present and the past. All of this fails to mention how strained some relationships became—some people questioned their partnerships, while people who were single felt isolated and ignored. And yet, with all the loss and all the uncertainty, many people found ways to grow and change and cope. And I'm not talking about mastering baking skills (though if you did, that's great too!). My point is this: No matter how hard things get, people find ways to be resilient—and even if it was only managing and barely making it through, that's good enough.

I don't mention the pandemic in the rest of this book. I want to imagine a world when the pandemic or other such moments of society-wide crisis won't be a burden on you—that this will hopefully be something in your rearview mirror, something that has been left mostly behind. I understand that scars from the pandemic or other disasters we might have experienced will remain for all of us. For trauma survivors, they'll be woven into already existent trauma narratives, even ones that are disjointed. Whether or not we lost someone close to us, it will take years to not only understand and digest, but to grieve all that we have lost. But resilience *is* a quality you can cultivate in yourself, to make even times of great adversity more bearable, and to strengthen and maintain your sense of identity and self-worth no matter what life may bring.

Setting Out on Your Unique Journey

Like survivors themselves, the experience of trauma is incredibly diverse. However, I do hope that many aspects of this book speak to you, help you feel understood, seen, and less alone, and that through the work we will do together, you will find your voice and reclaim your identity from the trauma that tried to take it away.

CHAPTER 1

Complex PTSD vs. PTSD

Julie is a woman in her late twenties. She is bright, charming and incredibly thoughtful and perceptive. She chose a nursing career that allows her to help others; her intuitive instincts about what people need have served her well. Although this aspect of her life is successful, her past haunts her. She grew up with disinterested parents, who often left her alone for extended periods of time when she was far too young. At other times, she was left in the hands of caretakers who did not have her best interests in mind. As a young adult, she experienced a number of difficult stressors, one involving a natural disaster that destroyed her home. There were also other incidents of relational betrayals including difficulties with romantic partners that did not respect her boundaries.

Although Julie has been incredibly resilient, she struggles with intrusive memories of things she would rather not think of. Though she tries to maintain a cheerful attitude toward life, at times she feels underwater with intense feelings of anxiety and depression. Sometimes she can even wonder if life should be as hard as it is. Though she has had many friends and acquaintances, she finds that people can be incredibly disappointing, yet she wonders if this is due to bad luck or if something is amiss in terms of whom she picks. Julie's thoughtfulness can also lead her to feel overly responsible for things that may not be her fault. And at times she worries her emotions can become too big and her expression of emotions too outsized for some situations. She spends a lot of time confused about how best to respond to situations in which she feels something is unfair, and it's never quite clear, in her own mind, if she has taken a needed stance or overreacted.

If you recognize aspects of Julie in yourself, you are not alone. What I have presented so far about Julie are just a few things that affect people impacted by complex post-traumatic stress disorder (CPTSD).

You're probably familiar with post-traumatic stress disorder (PTSD). You may also have been hearing a lot more lately about CPTSD. In this chapter, we'll explore what CPTSD is and how it's distinct from PTSD. A lot of people who have CPTSD symptoms can seem hard to understand using the older (and mostly male-dominated) norms in my field. As a therapist and a woman who has lived through trauma, this has been painful for me. It can be difficult for any of us with histories of trauma to know how to express ourselves, how to protect ourselves, and how to get what we really need. One major purpose of this book is to say that things are changing in the psychology world—the increase in interest in CPTSD is evidence of that—and your struggles are seen, they are common, and they can be understood. Moreover, even though your challenges have been hard, there is a path to feeling and being more in control of your life, even to reclaim the parts of life that have been taken from you.

In this chapter, you'll begin your journey to recovery from complex trauma by understanding what CPTSD is and the consequences it can have for you, as well as how you understand yourself, your own feelings, thoughts, and mind—which is the first step to changing responses to trauma, related patterns, and the effects they may be having on your life.

What Is CPTSD?

"Classic" or traditional PTSD happens when we experience one or two discrete traumatic events, or events that cause more psychological stress than you have tools to cope with. Complex trauma, on the other hand, involves the *aggregate of traumatic events* that have accrued over a lifetime. Many people with complex PTSD have experienced abusive or adverse experiences in childhood. Abusive experiences include the obvious things we consider when we think of abuse. such as physical harm and sexual abuse; it also includes emotional manipulation that involves caregivers exploiting their power, or what some people refer to as *betrayal trauma.* This is when someone we trust, someone we need, acts in ways that are harmful to us—even when they know better. An example might be a parent whose discipline is designed to humiliate us and/or to grant them pleasure from our suffering. Other difficult or adverse childhood experiences that can cause CPTSD include severe neglect, a household member who has been incarcerated, substance abuse in the home, a caretaker who was suicidal, and/or domestic violence.

Those with CPTSD often have repeated experiences of violence, trauma, or other extremely taxing events that start in childhood and which often continue into adulthood.

This latter issue has been studied in a variety of ways, but the shorthand way of expressing it is to say that if you have a traumatic history, you may be more likely to be victimized later in life.

Complex trauma has been minimized and not well understood. For many years, people who have experienced complex trauma were often told they had personality disorders, especially borderline personality disorder (BPD). This is problematic for several reasons. People who have survived complex trauma can feel that a personality disorder diagnosis doesn't fit because it implies that what are actually symptoms in response to trauma are simply products of your personality—which, in turn, makes it hard to get better. Also, labeling CPTSD as a personality disorder carries a stigma that negates how incredibly resilient trauma survivors are. Your coping mechanisms and the ways you cope with stress are often a product of the environment, *not* something that is inherently wrong with you.

Healing is about internal reflection as well as noticing patterns of a familiarity in being around people who may not always have your best interest in mind. To put a finer point on this, let's reflect on a realization from a client who has spent considerable amounts of time thinking about their life and their troubles, who told me: "I know I have a part in my problems, and maybe I do things that push people's buttons sometimes. But I realized that my issues are not just me; it's the people I surround myself with. I have people in my life who gaslight me or even don't treat me that well. And now I'm like, 'Wait, I have to deal with both myself and also what I allow myself to put up with.'" In other words, they'd suddenly realized that people in their life were mistreating them!

People who have survived complex trauma can and do get better, but it starts with realistic and accurate diagnoses, and a movement away from pathologizing. That work is happening, if slowly; although the CPTSD diagnosis is not in the most recent edition of the psychiatric "bible" known as the *Diagnostic and Statistical Manual of Mental Disorders* (DSM-5), it is included in the newest version of the *International Classification of Diseases* (ICD-11), which is published through the World Health Organization. Recently, many psychologists, doctors, and other mental health professionals have been willing to increase their understanding of the lifelong impact trauma has. But in the years preceding this shift, we let clients down.

Perhaps you've had the experience of a mental health professional who couldn't recognize the trauma you experienced. This often happens when the trauma wasn't the result of one or two discrete traumatic experiences, but instead relational in nature (based on attachments you have or have had). These are often related to long-term relationships you had, as a child or an adult, which shaped the way you connected to others (including yourself) for years to come. But this is also where you can be optimistic: Relationships can hurt, but they also can heal.

This workbook can be the start of that healing. It can help you deal with the complex trauma you experienced and the anxiety, fear, and anger you might be feeling, and start you on the road to finding true support by cultivating stronger relationships with others—and with yourself.

CPTSD as Identity Theft

At its core, complex trauma involves our identities. When we are young, we need a safe environment. This sounds obvious; it's not good if we don't feel cared for. But the result of trauma and other difficult experiences is that we become too distracted to develop a relationship with our own minds. What I mean by this is that adults who have not been repeatedly traumatized experience the world very differently than those who have. Typically, someone without CPTSD knows what they want and can make decisions about what their adult lives should look like. It may be easier for them to get along well with a variety of different people. They don't worry as much about what's on others' minds; they can enter relationships without much fear. They also typically know when relationships are **not** helpful. They can sense when something is not right and even when it's hard, they can leave, as painful as it may be.

Ultimately, the difference between those who haven't experienced complex trauma and those who have is the level of confidence in knowing what we think and how we feel. If we can think about ourselves clearly, we can take the actions we need to take care of ourselves. But trauma takes away the ability to trust your own instincts; this is just one way trauma robs us of aspects of our identity.

Considering trauma that starts in childhood, the "job" of being a kid should involve us learning how to handle emotions of all kinds, and how to distinguish what is on our minds versus what others might be thinking or feeling. When the environment is not safe, we can get distracted in a few fundamental ways. There are many ways the cycle of trauma can impact your sense of self, and these are explored in figure 1.1 below; as you consider the information in this section, assess which may apply to you.

Your identity and your sense of self are profoundly impacted by all the elements that surround it, as shown in figure 1.1 below. Here, an unsafe early environment, and additional traumatic events you might experience as an adult, can lead to fear, which can lead to hyper-vigilance—a super-sharp focus on what's going on around you and the threats that we feel may be present. Because of both the nature of traumatic events and the burden of CPTSD symptoms, anger is another common and understandable result. The weight of fear and anger are often linked with intense feelings of anxiety, which can lead to *dissociation*—a kind of collapse or fracture of the mind that makes it hard for us to feel our sense of self is coherent—which can trigger or worsen the entire trauma cycle.

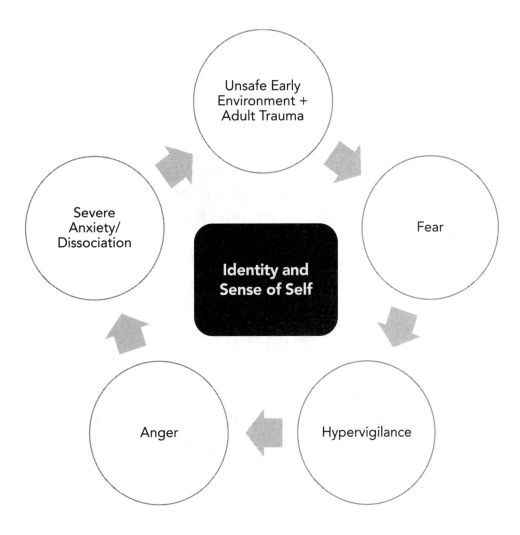

Figure 1.1. The Interpersonal Cycle of Trauma

Ultimately, both early trauma and repeated experiences of mistreatment make us afraid—in ways that never really go away until we deal with them. Fear manifests itself in many ways. Sometimes, fear can land more in the body, often through physical illnesses that can be exacerbated by the physiological effects of chronic stress and bodily hyperactivation. But it is also experienced in the mind through anxiety, anxious rumination, and the intense anxiety felt during panic attacks. Sometimes, we work to mask the fear we feel with hypervigilance—the tendency to focus on the external to keep track of everything going on in our environment. Anxiety can even be linked to dissociation, the tendency to leave one's mind during stressful events. (Dissociation can be particularly scary—we'll discuss it in detail in upcoming chapters.)

The fear we feel when we experience complex trauma can guide us to various kinds of coping mechanisms in childhood and adulthood. Some people who have repeated adverse childhood and adult experiences can get very focused on what other people are thinking and feeling. There *are* some benefits to this way of coping. It can be helpful for us to understand others, and this is the true root of empathy. It can also make for a great career. Think of how helpful doctors, nurses, lawyers, and therapists are if they really try to understand the minds of people they are trying to help. Or even an amazing hairstylist whom you can't wait to gab with, because you know they will understand!

However, if you're struggling with complex trauma, you may do this for others a bit too much. You may spend so much time thinking about what's on others' minds that you don't really know what's on your own. This is a way trauma commits identity theft—if you become solely focused on what others want from you, trauma can rob you of the chance to become the kind of person you might have been. And when you're frustrated or disappointed, you may check out even more, which can leave you ill-prepared to take care of yourself if things go awry in relationships. These things can lead us to have difficulty with the development of a strong and cohesive identity. To state it plainly, trauma makes us too preoccupied with others or the fear we feel to think about who we are and who we want to become.

Understanding Your Trauma Symptoms

The following exercise will help you assess your CPTSD symptoms as well as the impacts CPTSD may be having on your identity—your ability to know yourself. Check below if you have any of the following experiences:

☐ Feelings of shame or guilt

☐ A sense of meaninglessness

☐ Difficulty managing intense emotions

☐ Frequent suicidal thoughts and feelings

☐ A feeling of being numb and disconnected from others

☐ A sense of being overactivated and unable to calm down

☐ Periods of losing attention and concentration and "spacing out"

☐ Amnesia or loss of memories of events

☐ Physical symptoms, such as headaches, dizziness, chest pains, and stomach aches

☐ More substance use than you think is common/using substances to become numb

☐ Thoughts, memories, or images you try to not think about

☐ A pattern of relationships where you're mistreated, but have trouble leaving

☐ Exaggerated startle response—e.g., jumping if someone comes up behind you

☐ Taking more risks than seems normal for you

☐ Feedback or your own experience that you might be too angry, irritable, or defensive

☐ Mistrust in relationships, even when it's not clear you should be suspicious

☐ Overly trusting people who you know on some level may be dangerous

☐ An idea that you have had a number of bad things happen to you which you may or may not remember in detail

☐ Specific memories/flashbacks of traumatic events that you don't want to think about

☐ Experiencing yourself as uniquely damaged or toxic

☐ A sense of not being real or not feeling like a human being

☐ A sense of numbing and confusion that may lead to self-harm/self-injury/eating disorders

☐ Unexpected thoughts or memories of things you would rather not think about

☐ Nightmares

☐ Anger "blackouts"—getting really angry or blowing up, and not remembering it

☐ Difficulty knowing something that happened "really" happened versus a worry that you "made it up"

☐ A number of intense fears that seem excessive to you—e.g., worries about taking public transportation, a fear of being trapped, panic regarding going to the doctor or dentist, etc.

☐ Chronic or severe anxiety

☐ Feeling like a failure or feelings of being worthless

☐ Difficulty choosing a career

☐ Problems working with others or in groups

☐ A general sense that life has no meaning

The more experiences you have checked above, the more likely it is you may experience CPTSD symptoms. Of course, it's always helpful to check with a professional if you would like a formal diagnosis. Either way, this checklist is designed to get you thinking about the symptoms of CPTSD and how this may impact your life.

Assessing Your Experiences

As you may have noticed, complex PTSD involves symptoms of what we think of as "traditional" PTSD symptoms as well as things that might be woven into our personalities. Sometimes we may or may not be fully aware of some of these things. For example, anxiety and/or anger are often manifestations of fear or sometimes feelings we experience, but we may not even be aware of how anxious or angry we seem until we hear about it from others or have a therapist suggest it. You may not be aware that there's fear at the heart of that anxiety or anger, and that trauma you've experienced in the past plays a role in that fear.

Consider a client of mine, Jane. She's gotten feedback at work that she is not a team player; she herself has noticed that she tends to, in her words, "blow up relationships" very quickly when she's frustrated—but just as often, in fraught interpersonal situations, she spaces out, and there are certain interactions in the past she truly can't remember. For the longest time, Jane just thought of herself as "difficult" or "moody." It wasn't until we identified some of her past experiences as traumatic that she realized that before the events that would upset her, she was always nervous about something.

It may be jarring to learn that we can be anxious or afraid and not really know it, but it happens more than you might think. I have a colleague who literally jumps when people say her name or someone comes up behind her. She's not even aware of being afraid, but she looks terrified. Her heart rate seems to speed up as she will breathe more rapidly, and sometimes she starts sweating. She is not aware of emotional anxiety at all. It's just a part of who she is and how she functions.

This brings us back to the difference between PTSD and complex PTSD. People with PTSD have had a traumatic event happen to them, and they often remember it even if they are deeply troubled by it. When they act the way my colleague acts, they can likely link the behaviors (referred to as hypervigilance and an exaggerated startle response) as being related to a specific traumatic event. But people with CPTSD may not have this awareness. Since CPTSD impacts your identity, one impact may be that you don't recognize yourself as a traumatized person; you may consider yourself "difficult," "moody," or "troubled"; you may blame yourself for your problems, even if only privately and deep down. With such a negative opinion of yourself, you may find it difficult to understand your own thoughts, feelings, and needs—more difficult than it would be if you understood yourself as a traumatized person who has been conditioned to act in certain ways. As such, some people may have less awareness of their problems and the understanding that they come by these symptoms honestly—as attempts to deal with what started as external insults and threats.

People with CPTSD also sometimes have trouble knowing and understanding what is meaningful. They're often good at figuring out what others want—but this knowledge comes at the expense of not knowing what they themselves may need. Therefore, it may be hard to identify your own values and goals. What's more, even if you *do* know your goals and achieve them, you might not *know* if you're happy as a result.

I have worked with dozens of professionals with CPTSD. Many have told me they aren't sure why they pursued the career that they did. In some cases, it seemed like a good way out of poverty; others thought a prestigious career would make them happy, or maybe had people in their lives push them toward prestige. Whatever the case, they were deeply unhappy and felt that they did not *own* their lives. This is another example of how identity theft can impact people with trauma histories. Things may appear good on the outside, but internal worlds can be marked with confusion and feelings of being lost that keep you from being able to recognize what in your life is good, or keep you from feeling that what you've achieved is truly what you wanted.

One caveat to what I have described so far: People have a variety of symptoms for many different reasons, and not everything can be linked to trauma. When you have CPTSD, you may know on some level that things *have* happened to you, but what some of those things are may be fuzzy and unclear. On the other hand, you may very well know certain details of things that constituted traumatic events. Ultimately, the goal of this book is not to tell you what happened to you; it's not necessary to plumb your trauma to the depths to deal with CPTSD symptoms, or to relate every difficulty you experience to a traumatic experience you've had. Just keep in mind that people with CPTSD may not be able to link trauma to symptoms in the way that people with PTSD can—and for the treatment of CPTSD, this may not even be necessary.

My approach to dealing with symptoms involves working with issues and situations that occur in the here-and-now. For people with CPTSD, it's not always a good idea to go back and revisit the past. This can be helpful for some people regarding some events, but people with CPTSD have had several events that occurred over a lifetime. There may just be too many situations to think about—and in the end, going back and processing every traumatic thing is not necessary for people to get better. (I'll have a lot more to say about that as we move through the next chapters.)

Understanding How Your CPTSD Symptoms Are Unique

The traditional symptoms of PTSD involve four groups of experiences:

1. Intrusive symptoms, such as recurrent or unexpected memories of a traumatic event, including bad dreams

2. Avoidance symptoms, involving attempts to skirt feelings, ideas, or memories of trauma

3. Changes in thinking and mood, including difficulties remembering parts of traumatic events, loss of interest in activities that used to be meaningful, difficulty expressing emotions

4. Hyperarousal symptoms, such as irritability, self-destructive behaviors, and hypervigilance

Complex PTSD is comprised of the aforementioned symptom clusters of PTSD plus three additional groups of experiences—affective or emotional dysregulation, disturbances in relationships, and negative and out-of-control emotions that are often referred to as disturbances of self-organization. It's also helpful to remember that many symptoms have a socio-contextual element. For instance, how we're socialized according to our perceived gender can play a role in how regulated or dysregulated we may become. Think of the unfortunate but consistent example of how aggression on the part of those who are or present as female is perceived differently than it often is among those who are or present as male. People raised as female may have been discouraged from feeling or showing anger—which can plant the seed for dysregulation by making it hard to recognize anger when it arises or know what to do with it. Conversely, those raised as male may have been encouraged to show anger—maybe even in ways that aren't helpful or kind to themselves or to others. And on that note, for folks who are trans or nonbinary, their relationship to dysregulation vis-à-vis upbringing and perceived gender roles cannot possibly be encapsulated in such binary terms, and in many cases those gendered expectations may be a root of their own intense struggles. Furthermore, it's important to remember that systemic racism has contributed to increasing hate crimes and violence among many targeted groups. For those who are non-white, these increasing threats may contribute further to incidences of adult and childhood trauma events.

Triggers and Coping

Take a second to write down a few ways your emotions can sometimes end up out of control. For instance, are there certain situations that trigger you or rev you up—maybe out of proportion to what the situations actually call for?

_____

_____

_____

_____

_____

_____

And when you get angry or stressed, how do you typically cope? Do your coping strategies have consequences for your health or your relationships?

_____

_____

_____

_____

_____

In terms of close or even more remote contacts, people with CPTSD often find others to be excessively disappointing. It may feel like most of the people you know disappoint you in some way, falling short of what you'd hoped they'd be or do for you. At its worst, it may feel like relationships cost more than they could ever give you, or like there's no one in your life you can entirely trust. And though it is true that practically all relationships involve elements of disenchantment, these feelings can cause you to wonder whether anyone is able to be good enough. In these states of disillusionment, you may forget that there can in fact be relationships that offer more good than bad.

Ultimately, intrusion symptoms, avoidance symptoms, symptoms of hyperarousal, and negative mood and cognition symptoms can all contribute to negative feelings about yourself—with the result that you may have trouble genuinely thinking of yourself as an inherently good, worthwhile person.

So Many Symptoms…How to Focus on Healing?

As you can see, there are a great number of symptoms for both PTSD and CPTSD. It can seem confusing and overwhelming to know what to focus on! If you feel this way, you are not alone. Therapists have different ideas about and various ways of approaching trauma treatment. For instance, there are proponents of exposure therapy who feel strongly that addressing avoidance is a key to recovery; in this therapy you're guided to confront trauma memories directly so you can learn to endure the sensations that arise. There are also other clinicians who think the only way to heal is to go back and revisit early relational traumas, while others focus on helping you learn coping skills for what you're dealing with in the present. And the thing is, there is data supporting all approaches to dealing with trauma (though there is less research on how these approaches can be used with CPTSD specifically). I personally believe that survivors of trauma need to find out what approach is right for them.

Different techniques work for different people. The rest of this book will offer one way to think about dealing with complex trauma, one that's focused on helping you learn skills to cope with the CPTSD symptoms you're dealing with in the present so you can modify the effect they've had on your identity. This approach emphasizes what I think is the most vicious of crimes associated with trauma, identity theft—the way your symptoms may have robbed you of your ability to know who you are and what you want in life. We will focus on helping you develop emotion regulation skills and the ability to understand your own thinking better so you can reclaim your identity: your sense of who you are and what you want.

We'll also touch on some of the major issues you may be struggling with, like situations you may be avoiding because they're triggering, excessive substance use, and even times when you may feel hopeless and helpless.

As I mentioned before, my field has made a lot of mistakes in understanding where you may be coming from. And it starts with the origins of psychotherapy with Sigmund Freud and psychoanalysis in the 1900s. There has always been a consistent emphasis on getting trauma survivors—who, you may be surprised to learn, were Freud's first patients—to tell their stories. But the way he treated these patients has had long-reaching and negative effects, leading to psychoanalysis not becoming what I believe it was originally intended to be.

Freud initially reported that these patients, all women, had been victims of abuse by care-takers. But because he was treating the adult children of his colleagues, that claim did not sit well. So after his first book, he changed his theory to say that women who thought they were traumatized were just confused about the difference between fantasy and reality—he rewrote the histories of these women, and rationalized it. As you can imagine, this changed the field for a long time, and a lot of people have been hurt by not being believed about their stories of trauma and maltreatment.

However, Freud also made a very good point—he posited that the past is always relived in the present, and that our unconscious is always living out our traumas, whether we want it to or not. While my clinical experience has taught me that this means we can deal with feelings that distress us in the present without having to dig too much into the past if we don't want to, some of those who treat trauma have proceeded under the opposite assumption, and like Freud, often dismiss these stories as fantasy when they are shared, further traumatizing their clients.

The result is that a focus on getting traumatized people to tell their stories (which, again, is not always necessary or entirely helpful, especially where complex trauma is concerned) and a skepticism about the narratives of traumatized people on the part of the very people they trust to treat them have both been baked into psychotherapy since its inception. My hope is to repair some of the damage this has caused by providing a transparent and authentic way to help you with your suffering—one that focuses on the symptoms you're experiencing now, freeing you from the pressure to explore your past; that may or may not be available to you, may be too far in the past to be worth recovering, or may be retraumatizing to unbury.

Again, the unconscious is really always living out our traumas, whether we want it to or not. If that's true, and I do think it is, we can focus on healing from trauma by just dealing with our current relationships. Whether it's with a boss, our partner, our pets, the mailman, the clerk in the grocery store, or whatever feelings we have in the present—they all carry some resonance of the past. We don't always have to go back to move forward—but if we do, we will use caution. We'll discuss this more in the next chapter.

Conclusion

Trauma takes away your identity. It interrupts normal development and turns you into someone different than who you would otherwise have been. If we can confront the things we feel, like fear and anger, and understand how the trauma we've experienced drives these feelings, we can restore our identities to what they once were—what they should have been. This doesn't always require extensive trauma work, so we won't be covering that here, though I will talk about the next stage of trauma treatment later on. Instead, we'll look at how to understand what we think and feel, how to regulate our emotions, and how to build supportive and robust environments around us that can enable us to live the lives we want—in which we're healthy, happy, and true to who we are. In the next chapter, we'll look at how the body and mind respond to trauma, and how some of your feelings, particularly fear and anger are influenced deeply by physiological responses to difficult and taxing events throughout your life.

CHAPTER 2

Monsters that Haunt
Conquering and Exploring
Fear and Anger

By now you should have a sense of how the concept of complex trauma fits for you, and whether you feel that these symptoms interrupt your life in some way. This chapter will delve more deeply into two main emotions people with CPTSD experience, fear and anger. You may be aware of experiencing one or both emotions, but this chapter will illustrate that both these states of mind are very important and intimately related.

You have likely heard that trauma involves both physiological and psychological phenomena (things that happen in the body and the brain). As humans, we are also animals; our bodies and brains react to trauma in consistent and predictable ways via our nervous system. Analyzing trauma through the lens of what happens in the body and brain is important, as people who are traumatized are often repeating patterns that are laid down in our brain functioning. By learning the neurobiological process by which trauma is registered (wired into the body), it will be easier to understand why it's important to create a sense of safety for yourself, learn healthier coping skills, and build a strong community of social support. All of these are necessary to break the patterns that CPTSD has currently locked you into, and to prepare for what some people call "trauma work"—delving into memories of traumatic experiences. This work may or may not be of interest to you. But with insights from this chapter and the rest of the book, you'll be able to decide if trauma work makes sense for you.

First, we'll explore the fight/flight/freeze response—what is now more commonly referred to as *HPA-axis responses*. This is a more nuanced way of explaining the physical effects of trauma. To be clear, the fact that trauma can be explained using neurology and biology *does not mean you are stuck in the way that you are.* But it may mean you have to work harder when dealing with stressful situations.

After discussing neurobiological (brain- and body-based) facets of trauma, I'll provide exercises to help you identify and manage fear and anger as they arise in your life. This exploration may explain a number of symptoms and experiences you have. For example, you may wonder why seemingly small things can set off intense emotional or physical reactions. Many feel as if there is something wrong with them when it's actually that certain things in the environment trigger reactions in the body and mind. This chapter will explain how to manage anger and fear when they're disruptive. And later on in the book, we'll explore how, once you're able to manage them, you can use these emotions in constructive ways.

How the Body Holds onto Trauma: Fear and Anger

Stress is both physical and emotional. Stress triggers the body's fight/flight/freeze response by activating the sympathetic branches of the autonomic nervous system. This system impacts things we are not even aware of, like breathing and heart rate—things that are automatic. The activation of this response had evolutionary value; it allowed us to be able to respond aggressively or to leave situations when we were in danger (e.g., being attacked by a predator). When our senses indicate risk—for instance, if you're walking down the street and suddenly, you see a snake on the sidewalk in front of you—a signal is sent to the amygdala, which is specialized for threat detection, to let your brain know there's a situation you might need to act upon. For those of us with PTSD or CPTSD, the process of threat detection and the activation of our stress response can happen automatically. In fact, research suggests that we can be activated and not even be consciously aware of it.

Let's take a moment and reflect on how these processes may impact yourself related to your traumatic background.

Understanding Intense Reactions to Trauma Triggers

Consider a recent situation in which you found yourself really revved up. Maybe you felt startled, maybe you got really anxious for reasons that aren't quite clear, maybe you got angry. Or perhaps someone said something that caught you off guard. Write down what happened. What was the external event?

_____

_____

_____

_____

_____

What did you notice in terms of physical sensations or feelings?

_____

_____

_____

When you reflect on this event, did you **feel safe, unsafe**, or did you **not notice** how you felt?

_____

_____

Remember that whenever we are extremely activated (also called hyperaroused), it is caused by automatic responses of the mind, body, and brain—and sometimes we really can't distinguish whether we are safe or not. Despite how complicated your emotions may feel, it's important to keep in mind that a big part of CPTSD is physical. Knowing how your body, like all bodies, reacts to trauma is crucial to healing. This takes the blame away from you, the victim, and helps you understand that every time you are hyperaroused, there is a large component that is out of your control. By understanding this, you can learn to better manage your internal world and the various facets of your external environments.

The hypothalamic-pituitary-adrenal (HPA) axis is a hormonal/stress response system in which cortisol levels are impacted via neurological responses to stress. The stress response is based on genetic background, early-life environments, and current life stressors. These three aspects combined lead to bodily activation, the increased levels of stress hormones and physical symptoms we associate with anxiety (such as fast breathing, tension, readiness to act quickly). The stress response can be triggered too frequently if we've been through traumatic experiences. In fact, we may end up in a state of chronic stress that weakens our bodies.

The HPA-axis response is one avenue to understanding the increases in medical and psychological problems among those of us who have experienced child abuse and/or chronic stress and chaos in early life and that continues into adulthood. Let's look at an illustration of the HPA-axis.

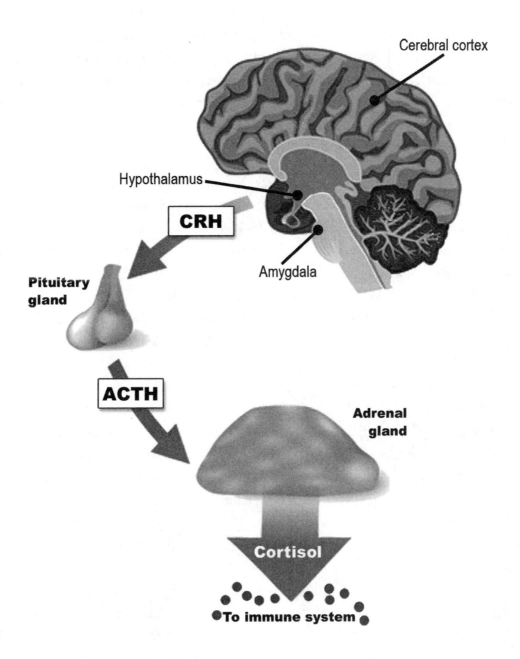

Figure 2.1. Brain and Bodily Responses to Trauma and Excessive Stress

As you can see, what happens to us has important consequences in terms of how revved up our bodies and minds are in reaction to difficult events throughout our lives. Knowing what happens inside of us can help us explain and be sympathetic towards ourselves when we are confused about symptoms, including thoughts and feelings. For example, a lot of trauma survivors can be troubled that they can't remember aspects of their past.

Consider the case of Daphne:

Daphne knew that she had been sexually assaulted as a child only because the person who molested her admitted to his crimes, leading her to be removed from her drug-addicted parents and entering foster care at age 10. Although foster care can be challenging, in Daphne's case, she felt lucky. Her first home not only took her in, they wanted to keep her. After her parents lost their parental rights, she was eventually adopted by her foster mother. Daphne felt close to her foster family, and her closeness with the family included a number of siblings with whom she was raised. She got a great deal of support to apply to college, which she completed with the help of scholarships, and landed a great job after leaving school.

But even then, as a woman in her thirties who had achieved a very successful career, Daphne struggled with nightmares, anxiety, and a sense of hopelessness. She had trouble with relationships, particularly with men she dated. She found that sex bothered her and she could get angry with men for even expressing any kind of interest. On some level, she knew this was irrational, yet she found herself frequently enraged once she moved in with her boyfriend. His presence, including his admiration of her, was cause for concern and considerable rage.

Daphne had had enough therapy to know intellectually that her responses probably were related to having been sexually assaulted—yet she could not remember this in detail, and so she always wondered if the assault actually happened. Her impressions of her early childhood were mostly empty, with odd but intense feelings of "blank spaces," fear, and confusion.

Not remembering all details of a traumatic event is a protective physiological response and not a sign that something is wrong with you or that what you think happened did not actually happen. Researchers have suggested that PTSD can affect the hippocampus (the brain structure that is partly responsible for memory). Several studies have found that people with depression have lower hippocampal volume; this may also impact people with CPTSD who experience chronic or recurrent depression. The secretion of glucocorticoids and norepinephrine that happens when we're stressed disrupts episodic and explicit memory, often making it difficult for people to have access to many details of traumatic events, particularly if their experience of trauma was chronic. This reinforces the reality that you may not be able to fully recall all the details of some of your trauma memories, particularly those from your childhood. First, trying to remember events may be very physically activating in ways that may be too much too bear. Additionally, people who have experienced trauma often feel pushed to remember things that have happened to them—which, as recent science indicates, may not even be possible—and this can put still more pressure on you as a sufferer. Therefore, you should continue to hold in mind the reality that healing does not require going through all memories of trauma; it may not even be realistic or possible to recover those. If, like Daphne, you struggle to feel that what you've been through actually happened to you, you should remember the notion of identity theft we talked about last chapter and the way CPTSD can make it hard for you to trust yourself—and you have to trust what you do know.

All in all, it's important to know that the neurobiological impacts of trauma result in anxiety and fear being part of who we are and how we cope with stress—and that this fear can be expressed as anger at others *and* ourselves. Appreciating the extent to which you may be feeling fearful and angry can help you begin the process of understanding and using these emotions to help reclaim your identity, so you can be the person you want to be.

Let's start with thinking about fear. The following exercise will help you pay a bit more attention to states of fear and how you're impacted. A lot of times we may not know how much fear impacts us until we are nudged to notice it. It's helpful to engage with your fear, as so often trauma survivors blame themselves for reactions or feelings they don't understand. Therefore, let consider the following: How does fear manifest in your life? How does it affect the way you act with those you love, and what you are and aren't capable of doing?

Identifying Fear in Your Everyday Life

The list below includes ways that fear and the anger it provokes can affect your life. Read through the items and consider whether each one applies to you. Check off the ones that do.

☐ You find yourself suspicious of people.

☐ You worry about being physically trapped in settings even when you know this is unlikely.

☐ You have frequent panic attacks without a medical reason to explain them (like thyroid dysfunction, heart problems, or perimenopausal symptoms).

☐ You get angry or upset quickly if someone implies you've done something wrong.

☐ People have described you as "wary."

☐ You worry excessively about what others think of you.

☐ You have an intense fear that people you are close to may die.

☐ You sometimes get feedback from others that you are controlling, or you have a sense that you try to manage others.

☐ You have a need for others to see things the same way you do.

☐ You experience intense anxiety or constant "noise" in your head. Sometimes it is experienced as "crosstalk," like people talking or arguing with each other.

☐ You have a constant sense of what others are thinking and doing.

☐ You worry that others will try to break into your home (even if you have good locks or a security system).

☐ You worry that someone might try to kidnap or harm your children or partner.

☐ You have a number of phobias about planes, trains, and automobiles, and worries when someone else is driving.

☐ You have a fear of driving over bridges, or driving in general.

☐ You experience excessive worries about physical health and worries about contracting illness (except in situations like COVID).

☐ If your partner or a friend seems upset or angry, you worry it's because of something you did.

☐ You worry a lot that others are mad at you.

☐ You find yourself wanting to fix others who have behaviors you think are not right.

☐ You worry that if you leave your children or pets alone with sitters, something terrible might happen.

☐ You have excessive schedules in place for your children in order to keep a sense of control over their safety.

☐ Being angry at others make you very anxious.

☐ You get nervous in large crowds.

☐ You worry others are watching you.

☐ You get really nervous or anxious when walking on a quiet street.

The more items you checked, the more likely it is that fear is a part of your life.

Recognizing fear and related thoughts is the first step to gaining more control over this common (and often unrecognized) emotional and physical state. If you are like most of us, you don't want to think about fear. Trauma makes it difficult to deal with any emotion that makes us feel vulnerable, and fear is one such emotion.

On the other hand, people who have survived trauma are often so accustomed to fear they just don't even notice how much it impacts them. This activity may have brought you into greater contact with the fear you feel. If so, this next exercise is designed to help you further practice dealing with fear and anxiety by breaking down what you feel into specific sensations and thoughts, so you can treat these feelings as the data points they are. We'll focus on fear first.

Confronting Fear

Try to notice when you feel fear. It may register as an upsetting physical, emotional feeling. Since fear often occurs in the presence of others, let's start by considering situations in relationships in which you may feel fear.

1. Think of a recent situation where you felt upset after an interaction. It doesn't have to be dramatic; maybe your boss recently put an unplanned meeting on your schedule, and it threw you off. What was the situation?

    _____

    _____

    _____

    _____

    _____

2. What were your *thoughts* related to the situation? For example, if your boss set a surprise meeting in your calendar, you may have thought your boss was trying to control you or catch you off-guard, perhaps something like, "She's trying to throw me under the bus." What were your thoughts about the situation you faced?

    _____

    _____

3. Did you notice any *physical sensations or emotional feelings* after the situation? For example, did you feel a pit in your stomach, or emotions like anger, fear, and worry? What physical or emotional sensations did you notice?

    _____

    _____

4. Ultimately, anything we feel becomes data that our minds use to make interpretations about the situations we're in. Did you make any interpretations about this data—both external (the specifics of the situation) and internal (what you thought and felt)?

_____

_____

_____

_____

5. In the hypothetical "surprise meeting" example, some people may have not thought too much of it. Others may have determined, based on their feelings and thoughts, that something bad was going to happen, like maybe they could get fired. What conclusions, if any, did you draw from the situation you went through?

_____

_____

_____

_____

6. After the event, did you wonder if maybe your reaction was a bit outsized—didn't fit the situation? Why or why not?

_____

_____

_____

_____

7. Next time you're in a situation in which you are fearful, what can you do to help manage your feelings, and perhaps achieve an outcome that's constructive, rather than one based on fear and anxiety?

_____

_____

_____

How you answered these questions will tell you a lot about how your mind and body react to stressful situations—especially when they're ambiguous. Feelings are important information. They provide us with valuable data, but ultimately our feelings are subject to our own reality testing; that is, they're often inevitably biased or provisional, and they may not explain all aspects of a particular story or event. For instance, in the situation with the surprise meeting, your instinct may be to feel fear that your boss is about to terminate your employment. But in reality, you actually don't know what the meeting will be about until it happens. And perhaps, when you take a moment to think about it, you can recall that your last several performance reviews were solid—and with this knowledge in mind, you see that it's unlikely this meeting is about your boss firing you. In our example, let's say that when you finally do go into your boss's office for the meeting, the situation turns out to be mundane; she is leaving for an impromptu trip the next day, and would like to discuss some business she'd like you to handle for her while she's away.

It's important to think about any reactions of fear and related anxiety as important information that ideally can be considered without judgment. The reality is that we interpret every situation we're in, and we do so in particular ways. Traumatic backgrounds often intensify our emotions and can make situations seem more dangerous than they actually are. Recognizing fear is the first step to healing. Knowledge is power, and you can use this information to help get control over your situation.

If you have identified fear, let's think about ways to help with this—starting with your relationships.

Strategies to Deal with Fear in Relationships

My approach is not to have you get rid of fear, but really be able to begin to be curious about it—and to understand fear less as an alarm and more as a data point that can help you get more control over your life, if you can respond to it constructively.

First, I'll list common examples of how fear manifests in everyday life, to give you some situations in your life that you might target as you begin to work with fear, rather than simply reacting to it. I've also left some space so you can jot down some fears that might be unique to you.

You notice fear when:

Your partner says something hostile.

Your boss calls a surprise meeting.

You get negative feedback at work.

You feel like a friend is not listening.

Your taxi or bus driver is being rude.

Someone makes a dismissive comment of you.

You see someone looking at you and you are not sure why.

Your partner seems distant and is unable to tell you why.

_____

_____

_____

There could be many things to add to this list, but just to get you thinking I wanted to mention a few common examples.

Everyone experiences people who may be aggressive toward them. This does not mean people are inherently bad; it just means that people we encounter will be aggressive at times. In fact, as I have gotten older, I've become convinced that everyone needs to learn how to deal with what we perceive as aggressive, in ourselves or someone else. I'll get to dealing with your own anger and aggression in a bit, but for now let's consider those situations in which you worry that someone else is aggressive—and find solutions to cope with them.

First, don't ignore fear. Let's say your partner is in a bad mood, one that suggests that they aren't emotionally available right now. Maybe they even seem mad at you. For people with CPTSD, this type of situation—common in all partnerships—can feel dangerous. It's important to recognize fear in this situation, because it can allow you to have more control over your behaviors and the way you respond. If you don't recognize and identify your feeling as fear, you may attempt to manage the situation and your partner too closely, trying to assert some control over them. This usually leads to conflict and often leaves you feeling confused.

Below are some ways we often respond that are *not* helpful:

1. **Asking your partner what is wrong too many times.** If you ask what's wrong and your partner does not want to tell you, it's usually better to back off and give yourselves both some space.

2. **Taking your partner's behavior personally.** Until someone tells you you've upset them, you have no data that supports your idea that *you* have upset the person you care about, beyond how you feel—which may not be correct. They could be upset about hundreds of things that have nothing to do with you, like hitting traffic on the way home from work.

3. **Escalating the situation to a fight.** People often provoke others to find out what is "really" going on in the other person's mind. While it's an idea that may initially seem to make sense, it may wind up pressuring your partner to explode. The outcome is usually better when you approach the situation more calmly and strategically.

4. **Not giving your partner space.** Fear leads us to pressure people for a kind of closeness so we don't have to be alone with anxiety about what we are feeling. Again, this is an understandable impulse—but acting on it gets us further from what we really want, not closer to the person we are worried about.

When people with CPTSD are confronted with an ambiguous situation—for example, someone else's bad mood—we fill in the blanks with worry that we might have upset or angered that person. These situations are hard to handle; we often feel as if we have to do something, to resolve something. These kinds of thoughts are a way to try to manage your own fear, because people who have CPTSD try to deal with emotions through others.

While this behavior is common, it doesn't usually work, particularly when we are scared. This leads us to act in angry ways ourselves.

Let's consider ways we can react to situations like our partners being upset with us, or someone we care about behaving in ways we can't immediately understand—which all boil down to the fact that someone we need and care about has done something to make us scared. What are some ideal coping mechanisms?

1. **Identify that you are afraid and know that this data is important.** You can't fix an issue you're having until you know that it's an issue.

2. **Take control where you can.** Worried your boss is mad at you about that meeting she scheduled? And it feels intolerable to wait until next week to find out why? Send an email to your boss stating that, if possible, you'd like to know the agenda for the upcoming meeting, and ask if there is anything you can do to prepare for the meeting or to help out beforehand. It's a calm, measured way to approach the situation. And even if you may not hear back until the day of the meeting, a compassionate supervisor might realize they should have told you what the meeting is about.

3. **Allow space.** Particularly in close interpersonal relationships, we can misinterpret the negative emotions in others as having to do with us. This is a natural worry, but one that can lead us down a path of trying to control and manage the feelings of others. Instead, it's often better to simply pay attention to signs of fear and hostility in others; and if you detect any, you can ask what is wrong—rather than trying to guess what might be wrong, or to behave in ways that you think will compensate for what you may think they're feeling. However, if the other person doesn't want to talk about what's going on, back off. Backing off doesn't always feel good. But it's often best to give others space; no one likes to be crowded when they're feeling emotional. Often, I encourage clients to reframe these situations in realistic ways. For example, instead of reacting from a place of fear—e.g., thinking, *My husband is angry. What did I do?* and pressuring him to solve your fears by pressuring him to talk—reframe it as: *My husband is in a bad mood. I have no idea if it has to do with me, but I don't need to assume that it does. And since he's being irritable and critical, it's clear he needs space.* You can even take time to reflect the situation back to the other person, perhaps saying something like, "I was hoping we could hang out, but I can see that you're not in a great place and that I may

even be irritating you even more. Let me give you some space and you can let me know when you want to connect." This demonstrates to the other person that you understand what they're going through, are willing to give them the time they need to sort out how they feel, and are open to speaking to them later and helping them if there's any way you can.

Think back to another ambiguous situation you went through recently that caused you to feel fear, and maybe steered you to behavior that didn't actually help you resolve the situation. What happened?

_____

_____

_____

_____

_____

Is there some way you could have behaved differently and taken control where you could, so as to approach the situation in a way that is calm and measured, not fear-driven?

_____

_____

_____

_____

Could you have benefited from taking or making some space—maybe by encouraging yourself and the people involved in the situation to take a break and come back to the situation later, rather than trying to control or manage their feelings in the moment? Or maybe inviting them to tell you what's wrong, in a way that's nonjudgmental and nonre-active, rather than trying to guess what might be happening and fix it? If the answer is yes, take a moment to write a script for what you could have said, and what might've happened afterward.

_____

_____

_____

_____

_____

_____

When we acknowledge our own fear, we realize we don't have to bring others into our own internal movie about what happens when people are mad or detached from us. We can recognize that we are safe, try to reach out to the other person in a constructive way if they're available for it, and create a distance from them if they are not. We can take control in the ways we are able to, not by pressuring another person.

As you may have noticed, some of what I have described in the exercise can also be related to aggression. For instance, perhaps when your partner is distant, you might react with anger rather than fear and try to fight with them to get them to reveal what's going on. However, aggression in CPTSD can involve far more than that.

When Anger Trumps Fear

Anger is a very complicated topic in both PTSD and CPTSD literature, and not well studied. It might surprise you to know that although anger is included in the criteria of PTSD, between 1987 and 2011 only 1.5 percent of research articles on PTSD looked at the role of anger and hostility! That's an incredibly small amount of research for what can be, for some, a huge and life-altering problem.

Anger is perplexing. It can be a so-called secondary emotion; for example, some people who are fearful instead express anger because it is easier. I do think this is the case for many people with CPTSD; their anger is often a manifestation of fear. And if you know that what looks or feels like anger in you is actually the result of fear, it may be easier for you to see how anger is the flip side of your fight/flight/freeze response. If "fear" doesn't feel like what you most often feel, it might be easier for you to recognize the anger you feel as a mask for fear, disappointment, sadness, and other emotions.

Some people with CPTSD end up entrenched in angry states of mind, and it may be that their only response to real or perceived threats is aggression. If you're in this position, it may seem like you simply cannot tolerate ideas or feelings related to being afraid, but it's often an intense fear of vulnerability and helplessness, and a sense of over-responsibility about bad things that have happened in your life that may keep you clinging to anger. This is because anger can feel powerful, as though you can protect yourself from getting hurt again. Attachment to your anger can also be connected to the idea of revenge and the belief that someone should pay for your suffering. People who've been through trauma may also feel an excessive need to control their surroundings, which can make them inflexible because change in their environment elicits an internal sense of chaos and overstimulation, which must be immediately stopped by attacking the source of their frustration.

You may recognize the latter scenario if you or someone you know seems "controlling." For example, consider Amit, who goes to his friend Steven's house for dinner only to find Steven hasn't set the table the way Amit would have. Amit finds himself agitated; he can't help but remark on the poor table display, and Steven can see how hard Amit's trying not to arrange the silverware the way he would have preferred it to be. This is an example of excessive controlling behavior. Something outside of Amit mirrored an internal sense of chaos, and he used the external setting as a conduit to try to gain a sense of control.

People who've experienced trauma come by their anger honestly. But it's not an ideal coping mechanism. It can alienate you from getting the help you need, and it can make you feel lonely and misunderstood in ways that can worsen your CPTSD symptoms. This next exercise can help you think about the impact of anger in your life.

Identifying Anger in your Everyday Life

Let's think about how often anger impacts you.

How many times a day do you get angry? Circle one:

0	1-2 times	3-4 times	5 or more

How would you describe the anger you feel most often on a scale of 1–10, with 1 being **mild irritation** and 10 being **extremely enraged**?

1	2	3	4	5	6	7	8	9	10

mild irritation   extremely enraged

How is your anger expressed and/or experienced? Circle all that apply:

I keep it to myself	I talk it over	Become irritated with others
Yelling	Throwing something	Thinking about it over and over
Screaming (e.g., road rage)	Crying	Feeling hopeless
Feeling depressed	Feeling worried or anxious	Becoming tired or sleepy

Other: _____

Have you ever worried that your anger was too much? If yes, why is this the case? Consider how you felt, as well as any feedback you may have received from others.

_____

_____

_____

_____

Have there been negative external consequences of your feeling or being angry? Consider work or interpersonal situations.

_____

_____

_____

_____

Have your wondered if anger plays a part in how connected you feel to others? If so, write about how this may be.

_____

_____

_____

_____

_____

Anger is a powerful emotion—one that society often tells us to diminish and to quiet, because it can be troubling in terms of how we function with others and ourselves. And this makes sense; we do have to limit ways that anger can seriously hurt others. At the same time, suppressing your anger, and not letting it out at all, can be damaging too—because if you don't let yourself feel anger, it never gets the chance to be known, appreciated, and eventually moved on from. Ultimately, the goal is to get in touch with your anger—and learn new, constructive ways to manage it, so it doesn't steer you to behave in ways that make your life harder in the long run.

One caveat: Though some more serious forms of violence can be observed among some people with CPTSD, many find that their aggression manifests in verbal diatribes. Ideally, we should strive to limit these as well—but for reasons other than the ones you may be thinking of. First, when we get away with being too aggressive, it hurts us as much as it hurt others. Not only does it tend to weaken our relationships, but most people who act in a hostile way toward others pay a price for this in terms of the guilt, shame, and even suicidal thoughts they can experience. So it's best for everyone to limit and manage aggressive impulses. That being said, I don't encourage you to try to suppress angry feelings. For one thing, trying to ignore feelings of anger and aggression can make them harder to truly address. These states of mind, like fear and all emotions we experience, are powerful data points that can help you to advocate for yourself, by recognizing that something's amiss in the situation you're in.

Managing Anger: How Fear and Anger Conspire Together

Now that we've seen how fear and anger operate individually, we'll look at what happens when they come together. Fear can turn into something that looks like anger very rapidly, especially in close interpersonal relationships. But I've realized is that sometimes we can take disappointing or confusing behavior from someone we love and *we* escalate it, before gathering our thoughts so we can talk about it. It's a very common dynamic, often designed to control our own emotions and those of others, and one that adds to confusion about our own feelings, especially if we act aggressively when we don't want to. Therefore, it's important that we think through these situations and act in ways that don't allow us to appear as the aggressor.

Let's break down a common situation. Jill notices her partner is grumpy. Jack tends to be pejorative and even kind of dismissive in such a state. Jill senses Jack is in a bad mood and she feels pulled toward him, instead of pushed away. Instead of providing space for Jack, Jill decides she needs to tell Jack of all the ways he has failed her. Jill's behavior *appears* hostile, but she is really trying to set things right in her own mind. She's worried. Is she the source of Jack's distress? Is Jack going to leave her? Is Jack not in love with her anymore?

But the main source of Jill's worry is often something like this: "Jack seems angry and I can't handle my own anger, so I need his anger to GO AWAY, no matter what." I often refer to this behavior as *outsourcing*. Jill may feel angry at Jack for being insolent—which is something our partners are entitled to be sometimes, just as we all are, but is indeed unpleasant to be around. Instead of managing her own anger and disappointment, though, Jill focuses on Jack's behavior. If she acts aggressive in doing so, and picks a fight, and then she winds up being the one to blame—what I call "holding the gun." So, I'd like you to remember this phrase: Don't be the one holding the gun.

I share this verbal meme with my clients when they tell me about interpersonal difficulties, especially ones that stem from their own tendencies to outsource their emotional needs and insecurities to their partners, as Jill did. "Don't be the one holding the gun" means you shouldn't turn a wrong you think has been done to you into a situation in which you seem to be the aggressor. When clients find themselves in these situations they may report only the last part of the story, saying something like "I blew up at my husband!" Only after I hear the entire story do I get why Jill acted aggressively. She was mad and scared about the way Jack was behaving and she took control where she could, by acting aggressively herself.

This less-than-ideal way of dealing with an irritable partner is common, but we can learn how to manage our fear and anger so that we are not the one who ends up taking responsibility for aggression that occurs in others. This starts with knowing when and why we are angry and trying to learn and understand what anger means to us.

Anger is an intense and frightening emotion. Most of us would prefer to be rid of it. But like all feelings, anger is data. It can be a valuable cue that something in your environment is not quite right. We need to learn to sit with angry feelings, without acting on them or judging them, at least initially—long enough that we can really discover what the feeling means; for instance, delving into the fears that might be driving the feeling of anger. To prepare for that, let's take a moment to understand how intense your experience of anger currently is.

Meanings of Intense Anger as Cues of Underlying Fear

Intense anger can occur for any or all of the following reasons. See if any of these fit for you.

I'm angry because:

- ☐ Of my own anger
- ☐ Of someone else's anger
- ☐ I am confused
- ☐ I feel out of control
- ☐ I want revenge for how I have suffered
- ☐ I hate that others have more than I do

☐ I hate that my life has been harder than most

☐ Others don't understand me

☐ People in power care little about my life

☐ There is not enough justice for real criminals

☐ Certain people get away with things that seem unacceptable

☐ _____

☐ _____

☐ _____

All the above feelings are honest appraisals of how people who have experienced trauma feel. You can learn from your feelings of anger. I want you to lean into angry feelings, with the intent to discover what they're telling you, and not to feel like you have to get rid of them. Some types of anger are often understandable—anger at injustice or at people who seemingly get away with horrible crimes is real, vital, and important to know and embrace. However, managing anger is needed if you get feedback that you are too aggressive, or if you find that the actions we take when you're angry hurt yourself—and others—more than they help.

Luckily, there are certain techniques you can use to manage angry feelings as they arise. Let's take a look at some of these techniques now.

Dealing with Angry Feelings

1. Be curious about anger. Feel it by remembering that no one gets hurt by our emotions—unless we act on them in ways that aren't constructive.

2. If the anger you feel is motivated by revenge or envy, just try to notice it. The way you feel is valid. It's not fair that others have had it easier; it's not fair that you're living with CPTSD. The key is to make sure you use what you feel in a way that serves you and does not hurt you.

3. Anger often signals that something may be sad and disappointing; try to imagine if you can hold on to these feelings of sadness and disappointment and come to terms with them.

4. Anger is often an emotion intended to help us organize how we feel. If you're feeling angry about something, maybe there is confusion as well. Try to see if you can untangle exactly what you're feeling and why.

5. In terms of angry actions, play out the scenario in your mind. For instance, don't send the vitriolic, angry email you've drafted until you play out how it may impact you. Remember, short-term satisfaction does not equal long-term gains.

6. Anger may not be noticed until it is in your body, so check your body. Is anger in your gut? Are you holding anger through muscle tension? Perhaps in your chest via how you are breathing? There are many different ways it can manifest in your body, so listen to what your body is saying to you about how angry and stressed you may be.

Conclusion

Anger and fear have an intimate relationship that aligns with the neurobiological aspects of trauma. Although these feelings can feel burdensome, they are good data points for you to develop a relationship with your own mind and body. Knowing how you feel is more than half the battle, and it takes a great deal of courage to own up to feelings of anger and fear. Remember, trauma is a form of identity theft. People who have not experienced trauma just go about their lives feeling whatever they feel, and they do not worry about the consequences—at least not quite the way you do.

As a trauma survivor, you do have more feelings to work through. This will not always feel fair, but it can make you remarkably resilient. You can own your identity and not let others define you ever again. You just need to know what you are feeling in any given moment, and assess the ways these feelings may help you or limit you.

In the next chapter, we'll discuss how to embrace and understand emotions without having to dampen them. We'll also consider how intense emotions can protect us and even keep us safe, while learning how to keep some of our bigger feelings in check.

CHAPTER 3

Beyond "Emotional Regulation"

Advanced Techniques for Dealing with Anger and Fear

If you have had therapy or read about complex trauma, you may have heard a lot about *emotional regulation*. The general idea of emotional regulation (or emotional modulation) is that we can manage our emotions by choosing not to be reactive to external situations or internal states and feelings. When strong emotions arise, we can notice the sensations and ride them out rather than acting on them immediately, or we can find ways to respond to them that are constructive rather than destructive. This concept can be important in terms of our well-being; it can preserve relationships with others and ultimately our feelings about ourselves. Let's start with an example that might sound familiar.

> *Shaya is single and deeply values her female friendships as a source of support. Yet, Shaya can easily feel angry and jealous of friends who have partners or a lot of other friends and she thinks a lot about where she rates in their lives in terms of her importance. Recently she felt like her friend Winter was being distant. Shaya reacted by texting Winter that she thought she was being ghosted and had no idea why. When Shaya did not receive a response right away, she attacked Winter with harsh messages, unloading her feelings about Winter in terms of the ways Shaya has felt hurt in the past. In time, Winter replied that she was surprised and sorry that Shaya was hurt; she then told Shaya that she recently has been distracted because something terrible had happened in her life that she has not had a chance to tell Shaya about. Shaya was left feeling sorry for her aggression, and worried that she'd overreacted and maybe even added to Winter's life burdens by not taking a calmer approach to addressing Winter's seemingly distant behavior.*

If this scenario is relatable, know that it's a common thing in relationships, especially when we're dealing with something like CPTSD. Often, we feel neglected, mistreated, or disrespected and then we *urgently* want to let the other person know how we have been wounded. And often, especially if there was genuine neglect or disrespect, our wish in these interactions is that we will receive an apology. However, people on the other end of these interactions can feel so shocked by them that an apology is last on their minds. In these moments, a difficult situation was made messier and more complicated than it needed to be.

To be clear, I don't want to negate the real sense of hurt that anyone of us can face in relationships. However, intense reactions can leave others so jarred that we may never get to what is desperately needed—a way to fix a relational problem. So, in this chapter, we'll look at emotional regulation, and how to respect and value our own emotions while still considering (as a rule and a practice) how the expression of our feelings may impact others.

That said, I believe that sometimes we *do* need to express ourselves in a strong and assertive way in order to set boundaries and take care of ourselves. We'll learn both when it is necessary to do this and how you can do it.

Let's dive in.

Defining Emotional Regulation

The American Psychological Association Dictionary defines emotional regulation as "the ability of an individual to modulate an emotion or a set of emotions." Essentially, emotional regulation is about consciously monitoring the emotions you feel, using your ability to assess what's going on around you to manage your emotions better, learning how to act on the information your feelings provide in ways that bring about helpful outcomes, and recognizing the full range of ways you can respond when you feel a particular emotion. Ultimately, when we're practicing good emotional regulation skills, the idea is that if something happens that triggers an intense rush of emotion (like anger or fear), we'll hold our temper and limit our diatribes against those people or situations that have upset us.

Your ability to manage how you express your emotions is important because it preserves your relationships; it also keeps you from feeling bad about yourself if you overreact or blow up at someone. There are inevitably moments when the ability to regulate emotions will fail, and figuring out what to do when you do blow up is as much a part of emotional regulation as learning to resist the instinct to blow up in the first place. If you react too strongly in a given situation, and don't have the ability to recognize and make up for what you might've done, you may end up in a situation in which people leave you. In the example of Shaya and Winter, Winter might ultimately decide Shaya just isn't worth her trouble. I'll have more to say about this in a bit, but for now let me focus a bit on why us not managing our emotions can hurt us as much or more than it impacts others.

Knowing and Learning from Our Emotions Protects Us

When we react too strongly toward others, it can make us feel bad about ourselves. We can worry that we are too powerful. We can worry we are too aggressive. In some cases, people can feel so badly about an outburst that it can lead to feelings of self-destruction or even suicidality. One of my clients, Susie, expressed this dilemma as "messing up her own bed." By this she meant not only hurting her relationships with others, but also worsening her own situation. After telling someone off, she would deal with terrible feelings of guilt and low self-worth; sometimes, she even wanted to kill herself. This was horrible for her—and ultimately, her self-punishment often did not fit her "crimes."

Like many with CPTSD, Susie was often way too hard on herself. Even in those moments we behave in ways we may not want to, such as being too aggressive with our friends, our partners, or at work, this does not warrant intense speculation about whether or not we deserve to live. Emotional regulation skills can help us break these patterns of self-punishment to keep us from damaging relationships in which we don't want to cause hurt.

When you think about managing emotions, perhaps you think about distancing yourself from anger, or downplaying it. Here, we'll explore a different approach: embracing our anger, so we can learn how and when we need to modulate our emotions, and when we may need to invoke a stronger voice with others in order to get heard or to protect ourselves. I suggest embracing anger and fear because, in my experience, people dealing with CPTSD frequently come to me with worries about their behavior and genuinely may not understand why they acted the way they did in the first place. Often, as we discussed in the last chapter, angry outbursts are a reaction to intense fear states—and if we can be mindful of anger, we can see if fear lies underneath the intensity of our frustrations and resentments, which allows us to really deal with what we feel in ways that are constructive, not just reactive.

The Tendency to Avoid Anger and Fear

Many of us want to avoid thoughts and feelings of anger and fear—even clinicians and researchers. Despite volumes of research on how to work with people with PTSD and CPTSD, many experts tend to ignore the importance of these feelings, or even their existence. As I noted in the previous chapter, few research articles on PTSD between 1987 and 2011 looked at the role of anger and hostility, only about 1.5 percent. Yet, among veterans seeking therapy for PTSD, for example, approximately 75 percent of males and 45 percent of females reported clinically significant anger symptoms. That's a lot of anger that isn't reflected in research!

As I've said, it seems what often can come across as an angry diatribe may be fear that is well disguised. But because fear makes us feel vulnerable, that emotion often goes undetected.

Perhaps one other reason fear and anger are so often downplayed is that both fear and anger can make so many of us feel ashamed. Sometimes this is from growing up in families where emotions of all kinds—especially ones seen as destructive, like anger—were discouraged. But shame often comes from traumatic events. For example, I once interviewed a number of people who had been in a mass-violence event involving an armed person who randomly targeted members of a large group. People who hid successfully had survivor guilt and other variations of shameful feelings. Some had never known terror like this and the awareness of the amount of fear they could feel made them embarrassed. Others, who did not realize what was happening and that people had been shot, felt "stupid," like they should have known better. Intense helplessness, like the kind we may experience following a childhood of repeated abuse and neglect, is also linked with shame. In these situations, survivors often feel, deep down, that they must have deserved to be treated as poorly as they were treated.

Shame also makes it difficult to think about traumatic events and related feelings. Therefore, outsized feelings are sometimes addressed as the problem instead of trying to understand the causal and underlying emotions. This can lead to survivors of trauma feeling blamed—like your feelings are the problem and not what has happened to you. It's important to remember that if you have trouble managing your emotions, you come by that honestly. People who have more experience in safe environments aren't burdened with the difficulties I am describing here.

Let's return to the more common ways we can get upset and risk blowing up a situation.

Using Anger and Fear as Valuable Cues

Take a moment and think about the last time someone hurt your feelings. It could be a close friend, maybe another parent at your child's school, or someone peripheral in your social group. What was the behavior that upset you?

_____

_____

What was your first impression of why they acted the way they did?

_____

_____

Did the event spark questions such as, *Is she okay? Did I do something in our last interaction that may have hurt his feelings? Maybe they are preoccupied with their job, marriage, or kids?* Write down any thoughts or questions you may have had. Or if these questions did not occur to you, just notice that without judgment.

_____

_____

_____

Did you take a moment to consider thoughts or possibilities like, *Maybe her treatment toward me has nothing to do with me? Maybe it does have to do with me? Maybe I'm not as important to her as she is to me?* Write down how or if you may have thought about whether you had something to do with the other person's disappointing behavior. Or if these questions did not occur to you, just notice that without judgment.

_____

_____

_____

Often, in these situations, the first step is just to question our intense reactions and then to think about what they might mean. These questions and thoughts and feelings matter. Of course, while some degree of taking perspective about another's situation can be useful, we can never know another person's situation perfectly just from guessing, so we should keep that in mind as we try to take others' perspectives in the course of our work regulating our own emotions.

Also, though it's often helpful to start with what might be our own contributions, it's important to also create space to think about how we are impacted by others. For example, let's say a hypothetical friend disappears when stressful things happen, and instead of telling you she's busy, she acts as if she wants to connect over text—but then ignores you when you say you've been sick with the flu. And then thinking about it more, you realize that when you do talk, she rarely asks you how you are, but spends most of the time talking about herself. These thoughts might be difficult to digest, since you want to think of this person as a close friend. And you could even see why it might be easier to blow up and get angry with her; it's almost easier to act up and feel bad about it—to be the one holding the gun. But if you make the focus on your anger or other feelings, you cheat yourself out of reflecting honestly on whether this relationship works for you.

Ultimately, the most important thing when it comes to regulating the anger and fear we feel, especially when it involves other people, is that we slow down, listen to our thoughts and feelings, and realize that if they are intense, it means something in the situation we're in may not be quite right. To be clear, having an insensitive friend is not traumatic; it may not even be troubling to some. We can choose to have all kinds of friends. Maybe you decide that you don't need another person who listens to your problems, but there are other things you like about certain people—maybe your kids are close friends, maybe you play tennis together and have a lot of fun when doing it. You can maintain those relationships as long as you're being mindful of realistic expectations. People without traumatic histories may not suffer the same amount of confusion when dealing with people in everyday life, but for people who have experienced adult and childhood trauma, these common situations can cause a great deal of suffering and confusion. Part of slowing things down is to realize that intense feelings of fear and anger *can* be helpful and likely have been.

Listening to Anger and Fear

Think about how fear and anger may have been helpful to you in the past. For instance, maybe you were out on a date and you had a bad feeling about the person you were with that turned out to be justified. Maybe someone openly mocked you and you felt you had to pretend you didn't hear it. Or maybe you expressed a need to someone or tried to talk to them about a problem you were having, only to have them ignore you or change the subject.

What exactly happened in the situation? What emotions or sensations do you remember feeling?

_____

_____

_____

_____

How did you respond? Did you assert yourself? Did you lash out? Or were you too overwhelmed by the situation to really act at the time?

_____

_____

_____

_____

_____

_____

Thinking about the situation now—especially considering what you've learned about emotion regulation in this chapter—do you think you would respond differently today? If yes, how?

_____

_____

_____

_____

Many of these situations are common. How we handle them is important, but more importantly is that we understand that in every encounter people we know are communicating something important to us. We need to listen and try to decipher the meanings of what people are telling us directly and indirectly. Our feelings of anger, fear, and confusion may indicate something does not feel right. Something not feeling right does not mean the end of a relationship, but it means there may be more in the situation we're in that we need to try to pay attention to.

Using Emotions Constructively

My hesitancy about some of the ways emotional regulation is typically taught is that because some approaches urge us to quickly diffuse intense thoughts and emotions—to weaken them or lessen their impact on us—they may also unintentionally rob us of the experience of learning what these difficult emotions mean and new possibilities for how to handle them.

In any relationship and in life in general, feelings of fear or anger may arise. It's important to notice these feelings and any thoughts that go along with them. One important mantra to hold in mind is: *Seeing something difficult in someone we love does not mean the relationship will end.* However, relationships are more likely to end when we shut off what bothers us.

Knowledge is power. This is especially true when the knowledge in question feels difficult to deal with. The complicated feelings that arise when we love or care about someone are so difficult that some people avoid relationships altogether. Or, if they don't completely cut others off, they might keep their relationships so superficial that there can be no chance of dealing with the messy and complicated issues that might arise. But the result is that they end up isolated from all the good that relationships can give them.

So let's think about how we might use fear and anger constructively when we're dealing with difficult situations. At its core, this involves noticing what you feel, accepting your state of mind as it is, and figuring out what you want to do next, without falling into traps like blaming yourself or others unnecessarily. Remember, the bulk of the work is internal at first. It's about how we use our minds to notice these feelings when they arise, see them as informative, and create space in which we can respond to them consciously and deliberately and not reactively. It'll take some time for you to learn new ways of relating to these emotions. Just keep with it; your patience will be rewarded.

NASCENT Skill Set

I use the acronym NASCENT as a way to introduce the following skill set. According to the Merriam-Webster dictionary, *nascent* means "coming or having recently come into existence." In other words, NASCENT reflects emerging growth and emotional development. It's the beginning of using our minds, physical cues, thoughts, and feelings in the development of an emotional lexicon. Noticing emotions (N) and accepting them (A) are key to healing from trauma. Staying safe (S) is a crucial reminder that when we get emotionally activated, we can all be at risk for doing things that can cause us harm. Considering (C) the context is always vital; we need to remember if we are in a more vulnerable state than usual when dealing with conflict and difficult emotions. Our triggers are valuable information. When we are reminded of traumatic events or having active PTSD or CPTSD symptoms, we can act in ways that we later regret.

Exploring (E) and thinking about the nature of our relationships is a vital part of this process. Trauma survivors are often stellar at forgetting what others have done to cause hurt. Indeed, you can be brilliant at forgiveness and giving people second chances. As hard as it is, we need to hold in mind both our contributions and vulnerabilities and what others contribute to difficult interpersonal exchanges.

We need to negate (N) blame on one side or the other and avoid all or nothing/black and white thinking as much as possible. Remember, it takes two to get things right and it takes two to get things wrong. Finally, *use your words* and talk (T). This sounds like a simple thing we say to kids when they are frustrated, but it's an honest and genuine call out to people who have survived CPTSD. It's so easy to feel quieted; it's so customary to feel like you can't say anything. But talking not only provides our literal and metaphorical voice, but it's also a needed way to reality-test our perceptions, and it's a way to set boundaries.

The emotional language that NASCENT represents, once it's strong and hearty, allows us to protect ourselves, learn from our internal and external experiences and enables us to consciously decide on behavioral steps. Below is a figure that breaks down each point in the NASCENT acronym. See if it's easy to remember this acronym as a way to stay grounded during periods of distress or conflict.

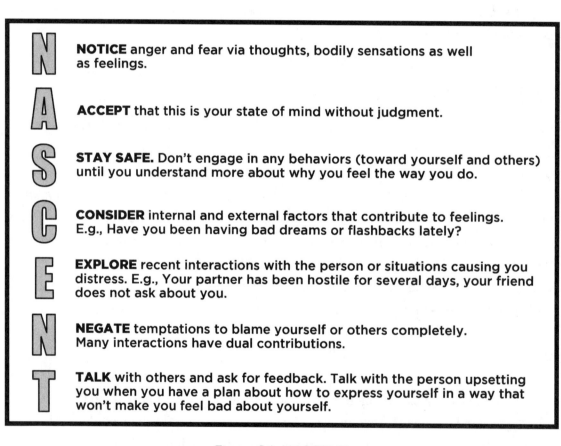

Figure 3.1. NASCENT

Keep in mind one way you may experience anger, or even notice it, is through physical sensations. In fact, anger often lands in the body before it manifests in terms of thoughts or conscious awareness. Therefore, it's helpful to review and notice the ways your body can provide data about whether you are angry or fearful as the first part of using NASCENT.

Physical Cues of Anger and Fear

☐ Dry mouth

☐ Shortness of breath/chest tightness

☐ Stomach upset

☐ Muscle tension in back, neck and/or face and jaw

☐ Sweaty palms or sweating in general

☐ Rash or hives when expressing yourself

☐ Dizziness

☐ Insomnia

☐ Flushing in the face or chest

☐ Increase in heart rate

☐ Uncontrollable expressions of anger, like road rage

☐ Exploding with anger in a way that feels out of control

These symptoms can indicate physical sensations of fear, anger, and related stress. (However, if these symptoms continue, please see a medical doctor who can rule out physical concerns, particularly if you have symptoms of panic attacks. Sometimes, these symptoms can be evidence of endocrine, cardiovascular, or even neurological issues, so get checked if you are not sure.)

Also, many clinicians have noted that having dreams of being chased is also an indicator of these difficult emotions. Finally, if it is not apparent to you whether you may be feeling anger or fear, pay attention to your thoughts. If you find you are worried about yourself or someone dying (when in no immediate danger and when no apparent severe illness is involved), or you worry a lot that others are mad at you, consider that these thoughts may be indicators of emotions you would rather not have.

The second part of NASCENT is to accept the thoughts and feelings you have without judgment. Remember, the thoughts you have cannot hurt people, so negative thoughts about both others and ourselves are normal and should be construed as valuable data we need to hold onto.

Staying safe means not acting until you can step back and gain perspective. This means not acting in any way toward yourself or others until you allow yourself to think about your actions and the behaviors of others and how they make you feel. Consider factors outside of your control—perhaps the person or situation disappointing you has nothing to do with you. Are you possibly more aware of threats recently due to flashbacks or nightmares? Is your nervous system revved up? If so, it does not mean that your feelings and perceptions are inaccurate, but it means take some time before expressing yourself. This will allow space for the next step, which is to explore interactions and experiences that may have led you to feel mistreated.

Rarely are feelings of maltreatment false. But we need to think about the context. Going back to the examples of a ghosting friend or a hostile partner, consider if there is a pattern in the hurtful ways this person acts. And if there is, prepare a game plan. How would you speak to this person about this pattern? How could you express yourself in a way that will allow you to say what is bothering you and to manage the defensive ways the other person might respond?

Developing a Behavioral Game Plan

All of this hinges on negating the blame you might instantly take on yourself or assign wholly to others. Since survivors of trauma often want to blame themselves—or, conversely, assign blame to the other person—it can make communication difficult. But life often involves a balance of complicated intentional and unintentional and conscious and less conscious ideas. When a relationship is more gratifying than not, consider that the good may outweigh the bad. No one in our lives ever gets it "just right." And if we're honest, all relationships involve some disappointment. However, if someone just seems toxic, and your relationship with them involves more pain and dysfunction than the pleasure of companionship and mutual support, it may be less worth expending your energy to repair it.

All the above suggestions should lead to a behavioral plan. How and when do you want to talk about your feelings? In many close relationships, the work is often more internal than external, but at some point, it may be helpful to say what we feel about how we have been hurt and how we would like things to change. This might involve setting some limits.

Practicing Expressing Difficult Feelings and Setting Boundaries

1. You've decided to say something to that friend who seems not to listen or to the partner who seems overly hostile at times. Set a goal for the outcome of your expressing yourself. For example, the goal might be to change the behavior of the person you are speaking to; it might also be just to let them know how you feel. Think about what you want, given the nature of the relationship and what you think the other person is capable of.

    _____

    _____

    _____

    _____

    _____

2. Consider how the other person might respond based on past data you likely have access to. How have they responded before when you have complained? Prepare yourself for how they might react. It's crucial here that you remember that they may get defensive or angry.

    _____

    _____

    _____

    _____

3. Be authentic and make statements about what you experience. We've all heard the idea that we should use "I" statements, which are a version of "When you did this, I felt…" This is less about setting yourself a fixed script for the conversation than it is about exploring the nature of the communication you want to have with this person. Be clear about feelings: for example, "I feel scared when you get drunk and yell at me." "I feel scared when you come home angry, and I

am not sure how to help you." "I feel confused when you say I am a close friend but you don't often ask about me." Write down your opening statement.

_____

_____

_____

_____

4. Consider how this person might respond to what you say, given what you know about them and common outcomes from the type of situation you're in.

5. Ideally the other person will say something like, "Oh, I'm sorry. What more do you need from me?" But this may not happen. Let's say the person feels upset by what you said. Perhaps they say they feel hurt by your complaint. This can feel confusing, and it can be a version of the strategy that's often used by people who abuse others when they're confronted about their behavior, DARVO: Deny, Attack, and Reverse Victim and Offender.

6. Although this acronym has typically been applied to domestic violence, even well-intentioned people can fall into the pattern it describes, since they may feel victimized when we complain. Yet, we are entitled to complain. So, consider how you might respond if someone DARVOs you. Let's say a person tells you something like, "I wouldn't yell at you if you didn't keep doing what you're doing." To be polite, you might say, "I'm sorry you feel upset, but I am entitled to my complaints and concerns. Just think about it, and see if you can consider some of my thoughts." Practice what you might say:

_____

_____

_____

_____

7. If the conversation gets too heated, walk away and give the person space. Don't do this in a punishing way, even if you feel the situation is unfair. Consider saying something like, "I see we aren't communicating well right now. Let's take a break and come back and talk when things seem calmer." Think about your exit and de-escalation plan.

    _____

    _____

    _____

    _____

    _____

Keep in mind that it is a lot easier to consider all this when you're not in the moment. But hopefully, completing this exercise will give you a sense of how the conversation might go and the opportunity to prepare for what you might encounter in it. Again, the trick is to be authentic, keep calm, and express your emotions without being too dramatic and or taking it personally, so that you're not perceived as the aggressor or the one holding the gun. If someone lashes out, it is best to leave the responsibility of their behavior with them, which we can do by not engaging in an intense or aggressive way. When we are pulled to react, we end up feeling responsible. I often coach clients in such situations to reframe the behavior of the person we are upset with as *They clearly need space. I'm going to respect that.*

In other words: If we sense that someone else has something going on that may not have much to do with us, but yet we are in the firing line (as we can all be at times in close relationships), it's essential that we let the other person know something to the effect of, *Hey, I get that my presence is upsetting you now and you have a lot of critical thoughts that may be about me. I want to respect your need to deal with your emotions. Let's reconnect after you've had some space from me.*

Giving Space and Speaking Your Mind

Deciding to speak to our anger, fear, or disappointment involves a lot of thought and consideration. So often, it's not what you say, but how you say it. People are exquisitely sensitive to aggression for reasons we don't completely understand but may have to do with our sensitive nervous systems. So, when we say we are providing space for someone who seems hostile, we need to be mindful of how aggressive we feel when saying it. In other words, try not to be overcontrolled with your speech—that is, pay attention to whether there's a subtle undercurrent of anger in your speech or your mind and body as you're speaking. People pick up on that and it can make them suspicious and even more hostile. If you are irritated, speak to it, but in a rational way. And if you're feeling emotions that are too strong for you to speak very rationally, tell the other person you need some time to cool off, and give yourself the space you need to process what you're feeling.

The burden on trauma survivors goes back to identity theft. Trauma survivors have to work harder than others to figure out whom and what kind of relationships they want and how much to put up with, while knowing that disappointment is an inevitable part of relationships. Adverse childhood and adult experiences force us to locate our thinking to the external environment, what we need to do to survive, at the expense of thinking about what we *want* or *need*. Thinking about it from a nervous system perspective, how stressed should relationships make you feel? You get to choose. You may need to wade through fear and anger in order to know who and what is worth your valuable time and energy. Sometimes we decide a certain connection is not worth the price. It does not necessarily get easier, but it does get more manageable over time and with practice.

Developing a Relationship with Your Anger

Fear is hard to deal with and it can take a great deal of practice to learn to acknowledge it. But anger is often even more difficult for many of us. And aggression is a very tricky emotion, and one that any survivor of trauma needs to come to terms with. That is, we need to develop a relationship with our anger that allows us to honor it for what it is without letting it take over what we do.

Anger is a part of life. For people who have not experienced multiple traumatic events, anger may feel unpleasant, but it does not often feel dangerous. For those of us who've experienced trauma, feelings of anger can feel too strong to bear and we may worry about the impact of our anger on others. This is often because of the relationship between anger and a sense of over-responsibility.

The feeling that we have been causal in the harming of others is devastating and painful in ways that is hard to describe and understand. Consider how veterans witnessing death or being involved in physical harm to others are more likely to develop symptoms of PTSD. This data is important; since the Vietnam War we've learned that involvement in military or civilian casualties is linked with a poorer adjustment to trauma following combat service. A version of this takes place among civilian populations too, particularly for those who have experienced childhood trauma.

This can be but isn't always linked to a direct reality of causing harm. Let me explain: As young children, thoughts are reality. Anger and aggression are important and needed aspects of childhood development, but children need adults around to let them know that angry thoughts won't hurt others. It is vital we learn how to feel anger while maintaining a sense that we are loved and accepted, even when our emotions can feel frightening and destructive. At times we may all wish to rid ourselves of people who frustrate us or present obstacles in our lives, often parents or siblings who keep us from getting something we want or command us to do something against our wishes. Think of a toddler who sees no reason to wear a coat when it is freezing outside and says to her mother, "I hate you!" A reasonable enough parent likely feels frustrated with this encounter, but also understands that her daughter is just expressing age-related developmental anger about being controlled. But kids who are being abused or neglected have more negative feelings toward people in their lives, and when these feelings can't be expressed—or, worse, the child is severely punished for expressing them—the child develops a complicated relationship with anger. In extreme situations—for instance, when parents are sadistic, or when a parent is especially envious of their child, wishing on some level that the child had never been born, et cetera—anger becomes a toxic emotion that can terrify a child, as if any aggressive feeling could kill them. And then there are instances when a trusted adult acts in a manner that's so egregious—like exploiting their children for some kind of violent aim, such as sexual abuse—that a child literally feels that they may die in the face of any intense emotion. Any of these scenarios can lead kids to become adults who can feel more powerful than they actually are, especially in the face of aggressive feelings.

Developing a relationship with your own anger, then, is vital to your well-being. Although identifying anger is important, I have found that what really helps us deal with angry feelings on a day-to-day basis is practicing knowing that this feeling is there and then experimenting with setting limits and boundaries with others. To be clear, the approach I am advocating does not mean that we always speak to our angry feelings. Sometimes, in close personal relationships, we may get angry or irritated a lot! When deciding to articulate anger, we often need to choose our battles. For example, I may see no need to tell my doctor she makes me angry if she does not listen; rather, I will try different strategies to communicate with her, and if these don't work, I may simply seek out another doctor who I think will listen to me better. It can come down to how much we want to exert valuable energy.

However, when we do decide to express ourselves, it's important we can get our message across. Our voice is a valuable boundary. Let's go over some points for thinking about our more aggressive feelings.

Welcoming and Constructively Using Anger in Relationships

1. Acknowledge that anger is an important part of your emotional well-being.

2. The more you pretend anger does not exist, the more it bothers you and can leak out with others.

3. Practice self-compassion regarding angry thoughts and feelings.

4. Remember that angry thoughts do not hurt others.

5. If you find anger makes you very anxious, practice saying to yourself, "My anger will not destroy anything or anyone."

6. Saying no or setting a limit is NOT the same as expressing anger, though it can feel like that. Saying no is a basic human right we are all entitled to.

7. When considering expressing your anger directly, consider how likely it is the other person will listen. Do they blow up when you express any negative feeling?

8. Humor can be a great way to express anger in a non-threatening way.

9. In very close relationships, it is important to be able to develop a language about expressing negative feelings. This can be addressed neutrally, such as normalizing the need to speak up when feelings are hurt.

The first step to regulating the anger we feel is to understand that anger is a part of all our lives and to come to terms with that fact. Second, understand that the more we ignore our feelings, the more they can haunt us; these feelings can leak out. The third step is to develop a sense of compassion around how angry we can get. One way to do this is to understand that, again, anger is often related to fear, though the two states can be confusing for people with complex trauma histories. Practice compassion toward the parts of you that can get enraged. Also consider that sometimes rage may be a mask for outrage. These two emotions are very different but can get easily muddled. Rage often involves intense feelings that can feel out of control with ideas of destruction. Outrage, on the other hand, involves a sense of being hurt and a sense of the unjustified nature of this hurt, and it's often paired with disgust. When you can recognize that you're not feeling rage, but outrage, you may be better able to determine when you actually *need* to use a loud voice to assert a need of yours that's not being respected or address behavior on the part of another that's hurtful in some way.

The fourth and fifth steps of this way of being involve reminding ourselves that angry thoughts hurt no one outside of us and that we need to realize that we can have angry and destructive thoughts and still feel compassionate toward ourselves for having these feelings. And not only should we be forgiving of ourselves—it's also important to remember that angry feelings are normal and a needed part of child and adult development. Angry feelings constitute boundaries and are vital to our mental health and our safety. The rest of the steps consider the importance of using our voice as a boundary. Our voice is only one kind of boundary. We can use other ways of setting boundaries, such as ignoring negative behavior or choosing not to engage in a fight. But when you do think about using your voice, always consider the audience. What is the track record of person you are going to speak to? If they have a hard time with hearing your thoughts, feelings, or complaints, remember that. Perhaps you can prepare them. You could say something like, "I want to talk, but I have some things you may not want to hear. Can you deal with that?" Of course, you are entitled to say what is on your mind, but it can be easier to get buy-in from the person you want to reach. Survivors of trauma can often *want* to believe that no matter the past, a current situation might pose an exception. Unless the other person is actively working on themselves, this is often not the case. So, consider ways you can prepare someone for hearing your thoughts.

Finally, consider what you want to say and how. Humor often can defuse conflict, though some people may find it shallow. Again, consider the audience. The main thing is to be authentic, and show humility if you can allow yourself. Let the other person you know that no matter how much you feel hurt, you still care about them and want to find a way to create a space where both of you can feel heard and understood. Pay attention to potential gaslighting. In interactions involving conflict it can be easy to provoke the other person or to be provoked; if it feels like the person you are talking to is trying to escalate things, remember that you don't have to be involved in a fight, or at least a fight that is not productive.

Conclusion

Anger, fear, and conflict are a part of life. Survivors of trauma have to work harder to figure out a way to deal with internal feelings of fear and aggression, and to realize that while allowing these feelings can feel very powerful and dangerous, we can all learn to use them to help us set boundaries. There is no perfect, prescribed way to handle messy feelings, particularly in close relationships. The focus should be on us being able to tolerate emotions, learn from them, and let them guide interactions in which we use our voice to set boundaries.

Even when we get very good at all of this, we can all still find ourselves in situations in which our emotions get the better of us. These are situations in which our trauma triggers can be too much, or our anxiety can get the best of us. At these times, we can be confronted with something that goes beyond dealing with anger and fear—situations which can cause so much fear and anxiety that we simply have to leave or check out, or dissociate. The next chapter will prepare you for these situations. We'll look at dissociation and how it impacts everyone—but also how it often is a more serious issue for trauma survivors.

CHAPTER 4

Identifying, Understanding, and Managing Dissociation

Dissociation broadly refers to a loss of access to or control over mental processes that under normal circumstances are available to your conscious self-awareness or command. Dissociation also exists on a continuum of normal or common experiences to problematic reactions that can interfere with our ability to feel coherent or whole. They range from the experience of lapsing into a daydream, to the ways we sometimes emphasize certain aspects of our personalities and forcibly deemphasize others, depending on the situations we're in, and finally to a more problematic kind of separation from yourself that can cause intense disruptions in both your functioning and the development of meaning in your everyday life.

In trauma reactions, dissociation refers to a defensive mechanism in which a person compartmentalizes and cleaves off memories of things that are traumatic. It's a method designed to promote detachment and keep us from getting overwhelmed.

It'll be helpful to understand dissociation in all its potential manifestations before we look at the ones that tend to be most common in CPTSD. I'll provide an example of a client who dissociated after a traumatic event below, but first I'm going to list some symptoms and traits thought to be related to this vexing coping strategy. This list is compiled from a lot of different researchers with varied perspectives on dissociation, as well as what I have seen in people whom I have worked with. As you read the list, check off any entries that resonate with your experience.

Indicators of Normal and Excessive Dissociation

☐ You have a tendency to daydream.

☐ You lose track of time in ways not explained by ADD, ADHD, substance use, or a known neurological problem.

☐ You're unable to remember the bulk of childhood and sometimes early-adult experiences.

☐ You tend to believe what others have told you about your experience.

☐ At times, under stress, you're unable to recall if dreams and reality are distinct.

☐ You often feel numb and foggy in a way that you cannot control.

☐ Your state of mind and emotions can shift very rapidly.

☐ You are very talented at becoming the kind of person you think others want you to be.

☐ You learn very quickly.

☐ You get very absorbed in everyday activities.

☐ You are very sensitive to the emotions and feelings of others.

☐ Many of us have clothes for different moods, but you have more dramatic differences in your outfits than most.

☐ You have a very active fantasy life (not sexual fantasies necessarily, but the ability to dream and make up stories).

☐ You may remember difficult things, but without a sense of continuity or narrative; memories have "blank spaces."

☐ You've had experiences of feeling outside of your body or mind, such as watching yourself in a movie or floating above yourself.

☐ You've had multiple experiences of feeling that things are not real.

☐ You've felt alive but also "dead" at the same time.

☐ Others have had to explain, in detail, events that have happened (in the absence of excessive use of alcohol or other substances).

☐ Your difficulties with knowing who you are have led to difficulties making decisions about what to do for work.

☐ You find that you don't learn from experience, particularly in relationships.

☐ You feel self-destructive when you feel someone understands you or "sees" you.

☐ At times, it's hard to distinguish physical versus emotional sensations.

☐ You have regular sleep disturbances, including excessive dreamlike intrusions while falling asleep (hypnogogic hallucinations) or waking up (hypnopompic hallucinations).

☐ When very stressed, you hear "crosstalk"—not necessarily distinct voices, almost as if a lot of people are talking at once around you.

☐ You are the kind of person who needs a lot of affirmation about experiences that have taken place.

☐ It's hard to trust your perception of events.

How many of the items on this list feel familiar to you? Keep in mind that this list is an aggregate of a number of different conceptualizations of dissociation; not all researchers would necessarily agree on these symptoms, and you may not have many yourself—but in my experience, these symptoms are common among people with CPTSD who tend to dissociate a lot.

You may not always consider the dissociation you experience a problem. So, it's worth looking at how severe the symptoms of dissociation you might experience are, and the degree to which you might dissociate now is one you'd consider excessive or not. Some of us who experience dissociation get along in the world just fine and may even find some aspects of this defense useful. Dissociation can be like a "magic trick" that can help us set a kind of boundary. When something bothers us, we just leave.

However, like all psychological ways of being, too much of any one defense can cheat us out of knowing important experiences we have had, including how to learn from them. Furthermore, too much dissociation can interfere with our quality of life. Not remembering certain events can be troubling; it can interfere with a sense of meaning. At times feeling "spacey" and "out of it" can get in the way when we need to pay attention. Also, sometimes excessive dissociation can place us at risk of further victimization, for example, when we can't access our minds to know when we need to leave a situation that is unsafe. Let's consider its impact.

Excessive Dissociation

Even though dissociation can have normal elements, there are some for whom dissociation becomes a needed and involuntary way of operating in the world. Dissociation often becomes a problem when we find that we cannot control our attention in the way we would like. It's in those situations that some people find themselves developing extreme dissociation and symptoms of dissociative disorders.

In dissociative states, it's as though you're leaving the situation you're in; your attention narrows in a way that becomes hazardous because it excludes basic aspects of experience. A client, whom I will call Sheila, described and demonstrated more extreme dissociation when she recounted a sexual assault she experienced in high school:

> *I went to their house; I was babysitting, was supposed to babysit for their five-year-old. I think she was five, maybe older? My mom dropped me off. They were a new family… I got there and only the dad was there? It was…weird. Maybe I don't remember. I did not see the kid. I remember, I think, asking what I was supposed to do. And then, it went dark, I mean in my mind… I was there. I saw the house and I remember talking to the man and then… I don't… I remembered walking home and how much it hurt to walk. It seemed weird and my mom did not ask me why I came home early. I just thought, maybe I made that up, you know, like some kind of dream… But I mean, sometimes, I think, did that really happen? Maybe it didn't…*

In her story, Sheila indicates the properties of dissociation in sad and tragic detail. She remembered some aspects of her experience vividly; in later sessions, she would tell me what the décor of the house was like and what she remembered about the details of an air freshener. But the assault only came to her in her bodily memory of the pain at the time and then later in vivid, but disjointed, recurrent dreams about the event. She eventually pieced together her story—she knew she had been raped and eventually could say how the specific event took place. Yet, she wondered if she was crazy—especially since her parents had seemed so unaware of what she'd been through when she came home that night. There are even marks of dissociation in Sheila's speech—the jarring starts and stops of how she tells the story, as well as what she phrases as questions. Sheila was there, but not there. She has protected herself from the violent aspects of her experience, but she knows they happened, nonetheless. In this way, Sheila's case demonstrates the reality that since excessive dissociation impacts memory, we can have trouble developing meaning of different experiences—even as some part of us may know or recall what happened. People with excessive dissociation experience disconnection from their own minds and a lack of continuity between thoughts, memories, experiences, actions, and identity. Sometimes, this means that a person who has been through a complex trauma experience can actually go back into the situation that was traumatic. For instance, Sheila later shared with me that even though she'd had some sense she had been abused by a parent of a child she was to babysit, she went back to the home and did in fact take care of the child on subsequent occasions. And in the end, Sheila could not really use language to make sense of her experience until she was in a safe relationship, with someone she imagined would be able to think about this event in a neutral way.

In my experience, some people with excessive dissociation, or who are grappling with past events around which they've dissociated, look to other people to fill in the gaps in how they feel about everyday events. Sheila, for instance, often did not know how she felt about everyday events, and she would seek copious amounts of advice from people in her life.

In a way, this was resilient; Sheila did not want to make any harsh judgments about people or circumstances in her life. She was also very smart and wanted a lot of data before making rash decisions. Again, this is a great coping strategy; we should all stop and think before we react. But for Sheila, this masked the experience of being hurt by others that was profoundly hard for her to take in, and so she did everything she could to avoid that. This became clear when her boyfriend had been seeing other women, something that was not expected as part of their supposedly monogamous relationship. Instead of having feelings about it, Sheila went to everyone she knew—friends, online groups, people in her church, all in the hope that they could tell her that her revelation about her boyfriend was not true. It was as if she wanted someone to tell her she was overreacting so she did not have to sit with the reality that someone she loved had betrayed her.

People with extensive dissociation can look to others to define their experience because they don't know what they're experiencing, and sometimes because there's something they know subconsciously or distantly but don't want to confront. And although we all need feedback from others, seeking out too much external advice can have its own cost. We may cheat ourselves out of knowing how we have been impacted by a particular situation or another's behavior. And again, we can be cheated out of aspects of knowing and owning our own lives.

Dissociation and the Loss of Ourselves

This leads me to define what I consider to be at the heart of dissociation, whether or not it is adaptive at times: dissociation is an out-of-mind experience. When we use dissociation extensively, we are not only *out* of our minds, but we are *in the minds* of others. This is often the case among survivors of trauma, who are typically clever, smart, and savvy. Dealing with people who have been abusive requires some level of figuring out what others want. This can start in childhood and be harnessed throughout the lifespan, as many of us find ourselves with bad actors at times, those who do not have our best interest in mind and who may have ultimately exploitive aims. But if we spend our lives figuring out what others want and contorting ourselves to fit those molds—which may be profoundly oppressive—we never get the chance to discover what it is that we want and feel.

Healing from trauma involves managing dissociation, learning to live with its challenges, while we slowly get to know ourselves and the contents of our minds, so ultimately we can trust our thoughts, perceptions and instincts. Let's take a moment to really think about how dissociation impacts you in the following exercise. No matter how you find yourself on the previous measure, consider the extent to which dissociation bothers you.

Your Experience of Dissociation

1. Thinking about the last month, how often do you feel you may have felt dissociated? For example, once a day, once a week, several times a day, maybe a few times a month?

    _____

    _____

2. Consider whether or not you were under stress before symptoms of dissociation (the symptoms could be spacing out, feeling foggy, forgetting much of an event, feeling a dramatic shift in your perceptions or state of mind, etc.). Intense anxiety can precede experiences of dissociation, so consider that as part of your answer if that seems true for you.

_____

_____

_____

3. Does the dissociation you experience disrupt your ability to connect with other people? If so, how?

_____

_____

_____

_____

4. Do you find yourself worried about states that feel fragmented or discontinuous?

_____

5. Do you ever wish you had more access to your thoughts or feelings? If so, try to imagine what this could look like. For example, "If I really knew what was on my mind, I would do X or not do Y…"

_____

_____

_____

Only you get to decide how or if you deal with dissociation. And if you are worried you may be minimizing dissociation or related experiences, try not to overthink. Dissociation is something that "works" until it doesn't. This is like many things in psychology; people do what they have to do to survive, but as we age and encounter different adult experiences and challenges associated with adult development (like having a child, getting married, a new job, etc.), the utility of certain defenses can change.

Again, there are elements of dissociation that are considered normal by some. On some level, we all have different personas that we present to the world. Like all things related to human functioning, symptoms are merely symptoms; if something bothers you then it should be addressed. And there can be benefits to being able to leave certain situations. However, this way of coping can become a problem particularly when it impacts our sense of ourselves, our ability to learn from experience, and if it leads to thoughts or feelings of self-destruction.

Managing Uncomfortable or Distressing Dissociation

If dissociation becomes a problem, it's often due to an awareness of memory problems, a desire for a more cohesive identity or narrative of one's experience, and/or feedback about behavior. Additionally, sometimes people begin to notice states of fogginess or "feeling out of it" that become increasingly uncomfortable. Again, I think of dissociation as something that works until it doesn't—and then it's useful to find ways to cope.

However, coping with dissociation is complicated, as there are many different manifestations of this way of disconnecting that can be addressed. Further, remember that dissociation can be protective. We don't want to get rid of it too quickly until other coping strategies are in place. And for severe dissociation (excessive fragmentation in identity), it's often ideal to find a qualified therapist who can help.

Below are some strategies for managing dissociation on your own and with the support of people you trust.

Managing Dissociation

1. Identify foggy states of mind. This might sound obvious, but feeling out of it can feel comfortable and familiar. If you start to notice this, pay attention to it. Does it feel pleasurable? Distressing? Just take note of this state without any judgment, and write it down when it happens.

2. Notice if fogginess or a feeling of being removed from yourself arises after you feel anxious or upset about something. Try to track events that may have led to this way of feeling with the following instrument:

Dissociation Tracker

Triggers for Dissociation (e.g., memories, flashbacks, nightmares, conflicts, fear, anger, extreme stress, etc.)	Type of Experience (leaving your body, feeling spacey, excessively sleepy, feeling not real, feeling cut off from the external world, shifting personas, etc.)	Responses (consider both adaptive and unhelpful responses, such as grounding techniques, asking for help, exercise, or drinking, using substances, cutting or self-harm, etc.)

3. Many symptoms of dissociation can be handled by grounding techniques. Grounding techniques are a way to bring us back into our bodies and the present. They are so simple and straightforward, we often forget how useful they are. Some popular methods of grounding involve:

   a. Finding friends who can offer distraction through activities such as shopping, playing games, exercise, etc.

   b. Using scents such as essential oils to stimulate olfactory senses. Rub the oil on your hands, like you would a lotion and take a moment to enjoy the smell.

   c. Touching something cold. Ice packs work well. Other options involve rocks/crystals with smooth or jagged edges. Anything that invites tactile sensations can work.

   d. Biting into a citrus fruit—the more sour, the more stimulating. Gum or a piece of hard candy is another option.

   e. Focusing on one thing outside of yourself and describing it to yourself. This can be a tree outside your apartment, someone walking down the street, etc.

   f. Putting on your favorite songs and focusing on sounds and lyrics, if you enjoy music, as long as it's not triggering or distressing.

   g. Watching a favorite television show or movie, even if you've seen it several times.

   h. Journaling. This does not work for everyone, but if writing helps, do it.

   i. Making a timeline of your experience of why you are distressed, in a way that works for you. (One of my clients made a Power Point presentation of recent events that led to her current state of mind!)

   j. Moving your body. If you exercise, do this every day. If you don't formally exercise and you feel dissociative, walk around and notice how your body feels.

   k. Going outside. Even if it's just going around your block or neighborhood or in your backyard, get outside and get distracted by what is going on in the world outside of your home. (If you can't go outside, open a window.)

l.   If you have to option of being able to work, consider that as a distraction.

m.   Guided mediation can be helpful for some. I prefer those that have body-oriented grounding techniques. Keep in mind that some people with trauma backgrounds find meditation causes too much anxiety, so don't be afraid to exit the mediation of this happens to you.

4.   Sleep and maintain a regular sleep schedule. Everything is worse when we don't sleep, but sometimes bad dreams and nightmares and anxiety can make sleep difficult. Here are some common sleep hygiene principles that can help.

a.   Schedule a routine around sleep. Try to go to bed and wake up at roughly the same time.

b.   Maintain a quiet and peaceful sleep environment; eliminate light, keep the room temperature comfortable (many people prefer sleeping in cooler temperatures, so consider a fan), and use the bed for just sleep and sex.

c.   Reduce caffeine. Old guidelines used to suggest no caffeine after noon. See what works for you, but I'd recommend limiting caffeine later in the day.

d.   Go to sleep only when you're sleepy, but consider relaxing activities in the 30 minutes prior to trying to initiate sleep, such as a warm bath or shower, reading, gentle stretching, or a guided meditation if that is not too overstimulating.

e.   If you wake up worried and nervous, write down things to worry about or things that upset you that can be addressed at a later time.

f.   If you can, limit screens 30 minutes before going to sleep. If you cannot limit screens, avoid distressing news and social media. Consider things on the internet that make you relax; looking at clothes or animal videos works for a lot of people. Some phones have wind-down apps built in.

g.   If you are having nightmares and cannot get out of them, get out of bed, and distract yourself. You can go get some fresh water and ice or take a brief walk around your home or apartment. This is not a time to think about the meaning of your dreams, but if it helps to move on from them, write them down to think about at a later time.

h. Get outside daily. Our circadian rhythms can be very sensitive during colder and darker months and/or when we are not sleeping well. Expose yourself to outdoor daylight, even if it's just a few minutes a day.

i. Exercise. If possible, try to get some aerobic exercise several times a week. Many studies find it helps with sleep. If more intense exercise is not possible, try to walk or do some gentle stretching as much as you can.

5. Memories, flashback and nightmares can increase states of dissociation. If you are in the process of trying to remember things, uncomfortable dissociation may be a cue to take a break from exploration. In fact, I often tell clients that if we are thinking too much about the past and traumatic memories, excessive dissociation is a warning sign to slow down.

6. Dissociation worsens with anxiety. Try to notice if anxious feelings come before feeling dissociative and try to monitor and challenge catastrophic thinking and work toward slowing down your thinking when anxious. It's equally important to find healthy ways to soothe yourself when anxious. Sometimes this can prevent dissociation.

7. Learn your triggers. What tends to trigger your dissociative behaviors? For people with trauma histories and dissociation, it can take a while to understand what can set off difficult states of mind, but consider that it can be almost anything—a song on the radio, smells, someone who acts like a person from your past, images on television, etc. Once you learn your triggers, eliminate them as much as possible.

8. If you can't eliminate all triggers (and really, who can?), try to develop an understanding of what is triggering and fight it off. For example, one client was triggered by cherry blossoms, as these were in bloom during an attack she experienced. She practiced noticing the flowers in bloom while telling herself that this didn't have to bring her back to her event.

9. For some people, focusing on gratitude can help. This can be useful, as long as it does not lead to a sense that you are not entitled to be upset. A balanced example of gratitude could be something like, "It's so amazing that I have a nice home given that I grew up without much money," or "Today is a good day and I feel secure and safe. That has not always been the case, but I am

fortunate to have this feeling now, in this moment." If you feel moved, write it in a journal.

10. If you feel that your identity is disjointed, remember that some clinicians have identified that we all can fragment into different self-states. If the degree to which your sense of self fragments seems excessive to you, consider finding a therapist who can help. In addition, I liken self-states as a team that can work together to help with coping. So, if you feel you have multiple versions of yourself, consider approaches that do not promote further fragmentation (for example, I avoid techniques that encourage the naming of "altered identities"). Work with whatever state of mind that you may be in.

Preventing Fragmentation: Managing Intense States of Anxiety

Clinicians and researchers still have a long way to go in terms of understanding the complicated phenomena of dissociation. However, there is general agreement that dissociation can be related to intense anxiety states. Although managing anxiety may not be a novel idea, it's important to remember how anxiety can be both a valuable marker of potential emotions as well as a huge limitation in terms of how we function. Again, I am suggesting that things we may have heard are problems can be viewed through a more neutral lens. Anxiety can be helpful, and it can be limiting. We can figure out how to develop a relationship with our anxiety so we can learn when it may be a useful clue, versus when we need to try to more aggressively mange it.

You may be wondering: How is anxiety helpful? When it comes to dissociation, recognizing anxiety can be extremely useful. For people who experience fragmenting associated with states of discontinuity, anxiety can be a warning sign. Anxiety can surface when people get triggered by environmental stimulation that reminds them of traumatic events. These include sights, scents, and auditory triggers. Additionally, many trauma survivors get overwhelmed in the context of relationships. People who disappoint us and have their own issues can be frightening and can remind us of times when we have felt unsafe. This can happen when people we are close to get mad, suspicious, and even anxious or depressed. These states of mind in others often have little to do with us, but they can remind us of times when we may have tried to figure out and understand those who have hurt us. It's important to remember that resilient trauma survivors are often very perceptive and receptive to the emotions of others. So, a trigger can be as simple as worrying about how someone close to us will handle their own difficult states of mind.

Although it may appear that interpersonal anxiety can be limited to those close to us, it's important to remember that social anxiety is also common among people who tend to dissociate. Social situations can require us to not only worry about how we appear, but to also can involve a great deal of stress, especially for the kind of person who is good at "shapeshifting" into what others want. Some people with dissociation can be quite good at figuring out what others want from them. But groups involve many different kinds of people, and it can be hard to figure out who to be when there may be competing ideas about what others may want.

Given all this, how can we learn to deal with intense anxiety in ways that are helpful to us and guide us away from unhelpful fragmentation? There are some tools we can use, helpful ways we can learn to detect intense anxiety when it arises and deal with it as data that can point us toward regulating and constructive behaviors.

Tools for Dealing With Intense Anxiety

1. Extreme anxiety is a clue that fragmentation is not far behind. When considering states of dissociation try to recall what happened *before* dissociating, both internally and externally. Did you have an argument with your partner? Did you have an interaction with someone that left you confused or uncomfortable? Did you have a memory or image of something that you did not want to have in your mind? Keep a notebook or log of times when you have felt foggy or disconnected and see if you can track antecedents.

2. For some, flashbacks can result in dissociation. Many people with CPTSD deal with disturbing memories all the time and are barely aware of it. When things come into your mind that you are not ready to think about, try to take control over your state of mind. An example would be noticing the memory and saying to yourself, "Yes, that happened. I'm not in the mood the think about it now. I'm going to compartmentalize this until I am in a safe place and want to think about it more."

3. Manage social anxiety by really spending time thinking about how often you want to be in groups. We may not always have a choice (e.g., work situations), but can spend time strategizing and planning regarding group interactions. If someone else in the group is also socially nervous, ask them to "buddy up" with you during the event. If possible, set a time limit on how long you will be there.

4. People with trauma histories are sometimes prone to feeling trapped. Think about your environment and *feel entitled to take control where you can.* For example, if you get nervous in windowless rooms, sit by the door, or ask a dining partner to swap seats if you feel uncomfortable where you are. The environment can make a big difference in how anxious you feel.

5. When anxious, use your mind to soothe yourself, if possible. This involves reminding yourself that you are safe now and no one can hurt you. I recommend that people literally recite the latter phrase. It's important that you not invalidate your feelings, however, since anxiety is a cue of present or past danger. If the danger you feel is in the past, then you can remind yourself that although it makes sense you have been terrified, right now, there is not external data to support that.

6. Flashbacks and many CPTSD symptoms get worse under stress. Knowing basic stress management skills is important to prevent "flares" of PTSD symptoms. Basic stress management involves the following:

    a. Diaphragmatic breathing, or belly breathing, controls and slows down breathing and can bring you back into your body.

    b. Social support with people we trust—be discriminating about who you talk to, but find people who listen and understand.

    c. Know when social interactions feel like too much and consider taking some alone time.

    d. Exercise daily if possible.

    e. Develop a sleep routine.

    f. If you sit a lot, get up and move purposefully every hour.

    g. Do at least one pleasurable thing each day.

h. Data on this is still emerging, but nutrition is increasingly thought to be linked with better mental health; consider increasing fruit and vegetable consumption, in addition to limiting fast food and processed foods.

i. Limit or eliminate chemical triggers of anxiety such as nicotine, alcohol and stimulating drugs.

The idea with these techniques is to appreciate anxiety as a warning sign while not being completely controlled by it. Flashbacks, dissociation, and many PTSD symptoms get worse under stress. And specifically, when you're dealing with dissociation, memories of trauma can cause fragmentation—so it's important to learn to manage anxiety and stress. I recommend you get grounded in the present before you do any deeper work with your past, if you feel so inclined.

Conclusion

Dissociation is a confusing range of phenomena that impacts trauma survivors. It is often a needed escape and defense when life is terrifying and unsafe. Dissociation should be managed if and when you experience it as a problem. Since anxiety is often related to dissociation, survivors can use anxiety as a valuable marker of information about what may trigger distressing states of discontinuity. Ultimately, the dissociation resulting from trauma is an out-of-mind experience. I think the best way to deal with dissociation is to slowly find ways to be more in one's own mind and to learn to tolerate the more challenging thoughts and feelings over time.

In service of this goal, the next chapter will explore another avenue toward healing and in learning how to access your mind—mentalization. Developing this skill offers a promising way to better connect with others, become empowered and in control of emotions, and develop empathy and humility towards ourselves while respecting the unique aspects of our suffering.

CHAPTER 5

Mentalization and Authenticity
Strategies for Metacognition

We are fortunate that trauma survivors have access to an abundance of techniques and skills that can help in alleviating suffering. To add to these, there is relatively new and robust research on what helps us heal from complex trauma that involves something called *mentalization*. In fact, some researchers think mentalization is a form of metacognition—thinking about thinking—and may be the main underlying principle to explain mental health. In this chapter, we'll explore what mentalization is and strategies you can use to cultivate this capacity in yourself so you can continue on your journey to reclaiming your identity and a healthy relationship with your own mind.

Another way to think about it is that mentalization is about knowing what's on our minds versus the minds of others. And as such, it's a way to combat the identity theft that results in too many taxing and stressful life experiences. When we mentalize, we avoid confusion, as we don't merge our thoughts with those belonging to others. It's an ultimate form of autonomy.

What Is Mentalization?

Mentalizing is a form of imaginative mental activity that allows us to perceive and interpret our own and others' needs, desires, feelings, and beliefs. It's an overarching way to *think about thinking* and reflect on our mental and emotional functioning. Although the concept of mentalization has been used to help therapists learn how to better help clients, these ideas can also be thought of as a form of ideal relating which can be taught and learned by all of us, whether we are in therapy or not.

Let's consider an example of healthy mentalizing and ideal reflective functioning:

Geetha and I had been seeing each other for a couple of years related to both childhood and adult traumatic events. The treatment was going well; she felt understood by me and we genuinely liked each other. As is often the case in good therapeutic relationships, Geetha experienced me as empathic, and we also had a similar sense of humor. This can be important in all relationships, but I have a dry sense of humor and sometimes people who do not share this form of humor may not understand me or even think I am being glib and dismissive. One day, she brought up an event she had spoken of many times before. She usually made a kind of dry joke related to the content and on this particular day she was feeling more vulnerable and sadder. As she described the event, I started to laugh, though I stopped as soon as I realized her state of mind was different. I had made a temporary but important miss of her mood and state of mind and she appeared hurt. I quickly apologized, admitted that I had misgauged her state of mind, but she left wounded. She started the next session by saying, "I've been thinking about that interaction and how hurt I was. You really seemed off that day. I was mad at first and I thought I should just quit because it seemed like you probably are just as sadistic as all the people in my life who've hurt me. But after a day or so, I was like, 'Wait a minute. Tamara has been understanding and I don't have evidence that she's sadistic.' And then I wondered why I reacted so strongly. You did pivot the way you reacted, and you even apologized! It kind of scares me that I felt for a moment like you were suddenly all bad. And then I wondered how many times in the past I have done that—not given someone a chance to make things right if they made a mistake."

As you can see, Geetha has done a lot of work on herself. She was not only aware that another version of her would not have given me another chance to connect with her in the way that she needed, but she could also come to understand that her reaction was outsized for the situation, and she was curious about why that was, even considering surprise, shock, and concern that she could suddenly dislike me so intensely. If she was not using good mentalization skills, Geetha could have come into the next session saying I had hurt her intentionally, with a collapsed sense of the differences between us—meaning she could have assumed that her idea about me (that I was sadistic) was true, because that was what *her thinking* was. And there would have been no way for us to think about the meanings of what happened and to repair the fact that I had hurt her feelings, albeit unintentionally.

When we have the ability to mentalize, it gives us a foundation to understanding our own minds and those of others. Mentalization is an ability that's crucial to various other aspects of being. The ability to mentalize is what enables us to behave in authentic ways, and to reflect about what we think others are doing or thinking in a way that's more accurate (as we can never really know for sure what is on the minds of others) rather than trauma-driven and biased. It also enables us to practice humility and to recognize and own up to what we don't know.

In this chapter, we'll look at how you can develop your ability to mentalize: to relate to yourself and to others and use that ability to build yourself relationships marked by healthy and safe attachments.

Let's see if any of these concepts speak to you.

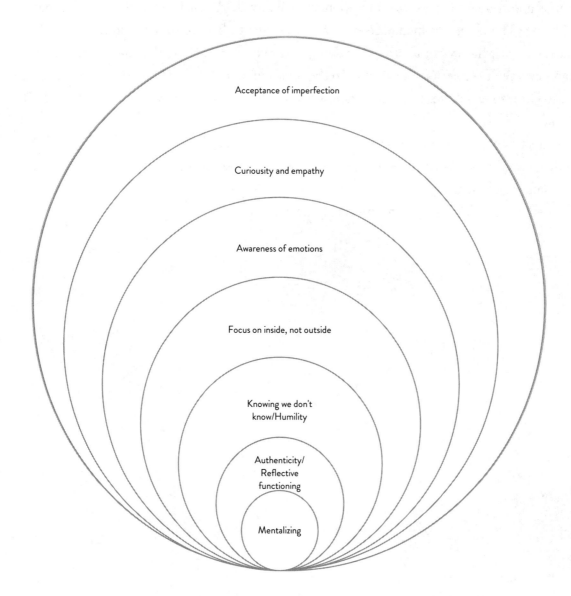

Figure 5.1. Important Concepts of Mentalization

Further Defining Mentalization

Mentalization primarily involves *reflective thinking* and *emotional authenticity*, the ability to feel and be genuine with ourselves and others—an ability that's also vital to mental health. For example, if Geetha had come in convinced I was a sadist, that could be evidence of a dissociative collapse (a more severe form of dissociation), which is the opposite of mentalizing. In dissociative states, not only are we unable to access the minds of others and recognize how they may differ from ours, we also can view others as bad actors and assume that any suspicions of ill intent we have had about them are true.

The principle of being authentic can help you remember the importance of having a relationship with your own mind and knowing and owning your own real and true voice. This is vital in fighting the identity theft that can be a part of surviving trauma. Part of this is *knowing what we don't know.* By this I mean two things. First, we need to approach emotional situations by understanding that we may not always know the answer to particular dilemmas and that we may need time to understand and reflect on our emotions, thoughts, and behaviors to figure out what to do. Second, in a general sense, we need to realize that there are aspects of our minds and our psychic lives that we may not always understand. Being *curious* about how our minds work is also a key aspect to genuine interactions in which we can be *humble* about our limitations. As a part of this, we often need to pause in our assessments and judgments of others, and ourselves.

This is why I emphasize that we try to increase our *focus from the outside to the inside.* As trauma survivors, the pull is to analyze the external world. In part we do this to assess safety. Sometimes, the focus on the outside is also a way for us to avoid knowing what is going on inside us. And sometimes, we focus on the outside because we can be fooled into thinking that anything that does not look like our past can keep us from becoming like where we came from. Without an internal focus though, we can't have an *awareness of our emotions,* and we lack the genuine curiously and empathy that we need for relating to ourselves and others.

And finally, *comfort with imperfection* is vital to our emotional health. Many people with CPTSD find solace in the imagining of a perfect world, one in which no one disappoints and one in which we get everything right. As we know, in reality, this is impossible—and understanding that is another key aspect of mentalization.

Secure Attachment and Mentalizing

The ability to mentalize is often defined by our early attachments, which leads to our individual attachment styles, as defined by John Bowlby and others. For instance, when infants feel unsafe with their caretakers, meaning they cannot predict how their parents will act and/ or their parents act inconsistently, they may go on to develop a *disorganized* attachment style as they grow older. Disorganized attachment is also described as fearful/avoidant attachment; it's linked with the confusion that results when caretakers can be gratifying but also terrifying at the same time. This specific attachment style is common among survivors of trauma, as well as people who struggle with suicidality and substance abuse. If you have some aspects of a disorganized or fearful/avoidant attachment style, you may notice that you may have genuine trouble knowing if you are secure or safe in any given situation and that you often worry that rejection, disappointment, and disillusionment are always on the horizon.

In contrast, people with *secure* attachment styles have a sense of security and safety growing up enough of the time—since no caretaker is perfect—that they assume that people will be relatively consistent in their behavior. As a result, they are not as disoriented by the disappointments and limitations in others. For example, an adult with a secure attachment style may be frustrated, angry, or disappointed when her partner is distant for a few days, but she can soothe herself by knowing that her partner will come back. Temporary abandonments do not lead to feelings of terminal neglect or devastating despair. Problems and frustrations in life can be solved independently or with the help of trusted and vested others. Additionally, people with secure attachment styles don't struggle as much with the idea of dependency, having learned that we all must be interdependent in order to survive and thrive in the world. For those of us with trauma backgrounds, dependency is much more fraught—it causes intense anxiety and fear.

Some researchers have described aspects of secure attachment that influence their approach to mentalizing. These aspects represent what we should strive for in our relationships, and involve some of the following:

- Reflectiveness

- Lively consciousness

- Freshness of dialogue

- Empathy

- Humility

- Little self-deception

- Ability to alter one's views

- Compassion

- Comfort with imperfection

These concepts sound reasonable enough, but they can be difficult to incorporate. There is not an external roadmap as such, but I always suggest that mentalizing and developing a good relationship with one's mind starts with being authentic. Being genuine and real, though, is easy to say and harder to achieve—especially for survivors of complex trauma, you can shift to become who others want you to be. This action is adaptive and protective. It also can be associated with great career success. Consider the case of someone I will call Jeff:

Jeff grew up in developing countries outside of the US as his parents had jobs that required them to provide medical services in different parts of the world. Dangers were present both outside and inside of the family. Externally, there were worries about the impact of sectarian violence. Internally, there was a parent, Jeff's father, who expressed rage and helplessness through violent means to Jeff and his sibling. And there was an ongoing yet silent knowledge that his father engaged in all kinds of extramarital relationships, often with those much younger than himself. Yet perhaps because Jeff was sent away to boarding school in junior high, he developed a great deal of resilience. He also proved to be quite skilled in computer sciences. Jeff went on to become a very successful adult who eventually led major companies and he was sought after as an expert in his field. Yet Jeff decided to seek therapy because he felt he had little sense of himself and who he was. He found he was certain of how other people felt, though. And while this led to some good decision-making early in his career, as he aged, he got feedback that he seemed remote and unavailable to his direct reports; they felt he judged them with little data. This troubled Jeff a great deal, but he genuinely had no idea what people meant when they referred to him as judgmental, distant, and remote. He was left bereft and confused by these complaints.

The Search for Authenticity

As Jeff's situation illustrates, one can be very successful in the world without being truly authentic. I find that people like Jeff often have a struggle regarding feeling real as they age, or as cultural norms change. In Jeff's situation, he had approached his career by being overly solicitous and "fake" toward colleagues and supervisees, thinking that the way to connect was to make "people feel good about themselves." Although not an entirely flawed strategy, Jeff had trouble during the #MeToo movement when some women he worked with thought he was being dismissive of their talent and was instead focusing on empty compliments. To be clear, Jeff did not seem to relish in exploitation of his colleagues—it was more like he was an immature adolescent, trying to figure out how to get people to like him. Trauma takes away the ability to have a relationship with one's own adult mind and thus, some rely on techniques that worked during childhood or adolescence. As a consequence, some people can believe that the way to cope in the world is to focus on what others want. In Jeff's situation, since he'd grown up with a father that was sexually inappropriate with women, he not only became confused about how men are supposed to act toward women, but he also adopted the persona he saw in his father, a superficial, vapid man who sexualized women as opposed to seeing them as equal human beings who may not be interested in shallow compliments related to the need to feel attractive. People like Jeff need help in finding a way to relate to people, and this starts with learning how to be authentic, which involves leaning into what we don't know.

Knowing That We Don't Know: Reflective Functioning

Authenticity starts with the realization that we do not know what is in other people's minds. A hallmark trait of people who have trouble mentalizing is a certainty that they know what others think. That is, they guess what others are thinking, and then proceed as though that's factual without interrogating whether it is, say by asking the other person questions or trying to empathize and see situations from the other person's perspective. Trauma, particularly when it occurs in relative isolation, often requires the survivor to make assumptions and predictions. Sometimes this can work. For example, a boy being mercilessly bullied in school can know that his bully is really out to get him. He may learn to avoid the bully and to arrange never to be alone with him. He may develop an assumption, "This other boy is mean and aims to hurt me, but I know this and I can protect myself." This is an example of how knowing something can be protective.

However, when there are so many threats in the environment, or when our understanding of what's threatening is conditioned more by complex trauma than by actual facts, we can get confused; we may assume threats are present when they are not.

Consider traumatic situations in which there are multiple witnesses. Some researchers noted that although the events of the World Trade Center attack in 2001 were devastating for those who went through it, there was something healing about having a large number of other people who could describe what happened and who could corroborate their stories. Indeed, validation involves the ability to reality-test with external sources, people who can tell you that what you went through was real. On the other hand, when you don't have anyone who can validate your experience (as in situations, for instance, when there is only one victim and one perpetrator in a room), you're left entirely to our own devices to make sense of what's happening to you.

Authenticity and meaning can only truly be defined by what we can detect from the inside. You *can* know what's real to you; you can't and shouldn't always rely on reality testing and validation from others to know what's true and what's not. At the same time, and paradoxically, true mentalization also involves the idea that at times you may not know what is on your mind. It requires you to sit with ambiguity.

If detecting genuine thoughts and ideas has been difficult for you, this next exercise may (hopefully) inspire you to consider your own relationship with authentic states and to learn how to uncover them.

Locating Authenticity

1. Consider the last time you felt strongly about something. What was it? What exactly did you feel in response, and where did you feel it in your body?

   _____

   _____

   _____

   _____

2. When you think back on this experience, how much did you consider what others would think of this view or value? Or did it feel like the thought belonged only to you? Consider how certain you felt.

_____

_____

_____

3. If others came into your mind in this instance, it may have been a pull to feel something based on someone else. If so, think about who this may have been. Let's say you argued for a view when maybe someone you are influenced by feels strongly about it (e.g., a parent, someone you admire, an internet influencer). If this is the case, label the other person's views and then label your own view. See if they differ.

_____

_____

_____

_____

_____

4. Switching gears, think of the last time you felt close to someone. Describe this in as much detail as you can. Consider states of emotional and physical feeling, such as warm, cozy, lucid, connected, full, clear-minded, thoughtful, insightful, etc.

_____

_____

_____

_____

_____

5. Now, consider the last time you felt disconnected from someone, even if it seemed like there was a lot of emotion or drama present. Consider emotional and physical states such as coldness, numbness, the presence of physical pain or tension, fuzzy-headedness, confusion, disorientation, a need to people-please, worry about another person's perception, anxiety, etc.

_____

_____

_____

6. Now, let's focus on when you are alone. What are thoughts that make you feel safe and like you have access to a core identity? These thoughts could be about people you love, people who have been there for you in a real way, people who know you well and care for you. They can also be related to your strength and resilience, and your ability to know your own goals and values.

_____

_____

_____

_____

7. Next, consider the last time you tried to please someone by becoming who you thought they wanted you to be. Did you say or do something you did not really want to? On some level, it may have felt "tried on" but "not really you." Maybe a friend complained about a mutual friend; let's say you did not really feel the same way, yet you chimed in—because you thought that would be a required response.

_____

_____

_____

_____

8. Finally, just sit with your responses to these questions. Take a moment to think about your core values and beliefs and what makes you uniquely and importantly human. Consider your values based on the following dimensions and check what matters most to you.

    ☐ Work or contribution to society

    ☐ The kinds of relationships you want to have

    ☐ Your relationship to your body and how you want to care for it

    ☐ The presence or absence of spiritual beliefs and their place in your life

    ☐ The importance of your own survival

    ☐ Feeling a sense of agency and control in your own life

    ☐ Finding pleasure in everyday moments

    ☐ Providing love and safety to children or animals who need you

9. Write down other values that make you feel genuine and real.

    _____

    _____

    _____

    _____

How did you feel doing this exercise? Hopefully it nudged you to think about your own values and beliefs as well as the importance of differentiating your thoughts from the thoughts of others.

Feeling and being real and authentic takes practice and patience, and acknowledging what works for you—like trying on different outfits to see if they fit you or not. I don't mean this analogy to be superficial, of course! Discovering what is authentic to us and feels right is often a long process of trial and error. We often do need to imagine different ideas as if they are a part of us, so to speak, so we can see what feels real.

Focusing on the Inside, Not the Outside: Managing Hypervigilance

Another vital aspect to healing from complex trauma is finding a balance between focusing on what is internal as opposed to what is external: working with the instinct of hypervigilance. Hypervigilance is a response to constant threats of danger and something we see a lot in people who have PTSD and CPTSD. It, too, involves paying attention to something outside of us, including what is in the minds of others, in a way that can start off as adaptive but become excessive. Over time, hypervigilance can become a failed cognitive strategy because there are simply so many things outside of our own minds to keep track of—it's impossible to keep track of everything. Therefore, there is an economic argument for us developing the ability to mentalize and to know what is on our own minds. We have *more control* over our lives if we can focus on what *we* think and then see if those thoughts match external experiences.

This leads to the next aspect of mentalization we'll discuss, which is knowing how we feel and being able to detect emotions without judgment.

Detecting and Owning Emotions

Knowing and detection of emotions is another important step in metacognition. But it's much easier to say "This is important" than to actually do it. Do realize that the majority of us do not really know what we are feeling at the time of an intense interaction. Knowing *what* we feel takes a lot of practice and a lot of work. If you have experienced complex trauma, then you are likely programed to leave your true feelings "at the door" when being involved in ostensibly emotional conversations—to put how you feel to one side so you can deal with what feels like a threat. There are ways to practice detecting and knowing your emotions—and definite benefits to doing so, when it comes to getting your needs met and achieving relationships with others that are healthy and nurturing, not driven by fear or uncertainty or kept deliberately shallow or distant. Try out these practices; see if any can work for you.

Detecting Emotions

1. The first step when you want to detect an emotion you're feeling is to check in with your body; emotions often land here first. Consider the last tense or difficult emotional interaction that you have had. Did it land in your body? If so, where?

    _____

    _____

    _____

2. The next step is to take a minute when you feel tempted to react to something difficult—just stop whatever you're doing and consider what is in your mind. Anger, fear, confusion? Think back to the situation you just wrote about. What was on your mind as you felt the sensations that arose? Notice this without judgment and write down what you felt or noticed.

    _____

    _____

    _____

    _____

3. You'll also want to practice knowing how you feel when things are calm. So: Think about how you're feeling right now. If you feel safe, notice that and consider what this moment feels like. If you feel anxious, welcome this without judgment, then ask yourself what you might be nervous or anxious about. If nothing comes to mind, don't judge it, but do try to be curious about your experience and note whatever you do notice or feel here.

    _____

    _____

    _____

4. When you have strong feelings, try to accept them without judgment. Remember, when we are kids, we need people to tell us that the strong feelings we might feel can't actually hurt anyone. If we don't hear this message, we may worry that our big feelings are dangerous, that they can put us at risk or make us threatening. If you did not have this experience of validation as a child, you must now do this for yourself. It may be hard, but just open yourself up to intense feelings, without feeling pressured to act. Write down any strong feelings you have had—and remember, feelings are neutral data points.

_____

_____

_____

_____

_____

There are no exact formulas for knowing how to detect authentic emotions, but hopefully this exercise showed you that there are some basic strategies you can use. To sum up the previous exercise, remember to:

1. Check in with your body, where emotions are typically first felt.

2. Know how you feel when you're calm, so you have a baseline from which to assess when you're feeling strong emotions when those arise.

3. Accept intense emotions when they arise without judgment, rather than seeing them as threats you need to suppress or shut yourself off from.

Practice is key. Remember that people with complex trauma, who often had to be conduits for the emotions of others, may get confused about which emotions are their own. Consider also that this feeling of being separate from others—painful though it can be—can also be the start of finding access to your own mind. To do this though, you'll have to work with and limit your hypervigilance, and see what comes up when you are focusing on yourself and not others.

Let's look at other ways you can build curiosity and empathy toward yourself and others, as you continue working to detect and know your own emotions and recognize your own experience.

Curiosity and Empathy Toward Self and Others

A key facet of mentalizing is building curiosity and empathy toward yourself and toward others. Now you might be wisely asking about how curiosity and empathy toward others can be useful—especially if you are someone who has relied on hypervigilance and the caretaking behaviors that can go along with that. Or you might be asking, how can you NOT be curious if you've been so externally focused? It's a good question, but think of it this way: When we are hypervigilantly focused on others, we're often focused on signs of apparent danger, and so we often miss key facets of what might be going on—like the old analogy of "you can't see the forest for the trees." In other words, if we are only watching for signs of danger in others, we unintentionally miss nuances of their emotions, as well as our own. Ultimately, hypervigilance and constantly paying attention to others may keep us from some threats, but we will miss the overall emotions in those we care about.

Again, this starts with curiosity, which takes some time and practice to build. Below are some strategies for practicing replacing the tendency toward anxious hypervigilance with realistic curiosity and empathy. Let's see if any of these strategies seem like helpful ones you'd want to try.

Strategies to Practice Curiosity and Empathy

1. When you have a strong emotion, stop and just consider why you feel the way you do, considering both internal factors (e.g., physical and mental sensations, your mood, your experience that day, a past experience or something you learned that you may be bringing to the current experience) and external factors (e.g., what the other person may or may not have done, the situation you're both in and the pressures you may be facing).

2. Remember, you do not have to make a case in a court where your feelings are considered valid. Feelings are genuinely valid, even when they're strong or when you feel that yours may not be entirely justified. So, allow yourself to be kind to yourself, no matter what you feel. And again, think of your feelings as data points that can provide you with valuable information while you *choose* how to react in the situation you happen to be in.

3. When others have feelings or thoughts you don't understand, take a minute and don't feel pressured to act as if you know what they mean. Ask questions. Even if some time in the conversation goes by and you find you don't understand what has been said, feel free to say something like, "Sorry, I think I may have missed the importance of something you said a couple of minutes ago, what did you mean when you said…?"

4. For many people with trauma histories, it can seem easy to be empathic, but remember that true empathy means considering as many factors as possible to explain a particular experience. If something in a situation or in another person's behavior seems obvious to you, pause and consider other explanations. What you're feeling may be founded in truth, but it's important to assess situations completely.

5. Practice imagining what someone else's experience is like. Even if they are very different from you, imagine what it must be like to be them.

6. Self-compassion and empathy are contagious. As you feel more in these ways about yourself you may notice you start to feel so toward others.

For the next week or so, try to pay particular attention to moments in your life when you can use one of these strategies. If you use any, write down the responses or thoughts you had:

- Stop and consider *why* you feel the way you do instead of reacting instinctively to a strong emotion. What did you notice?

_____

_____

_____

- Think of your feelings, even strong ones, as data points, not something you have to defend—and using them, choose how to respond to the situation you're in. Consider practicing reframing a strong emotion here. For example, "I felt enraged when my girlfriend did not text me back right away, but then I remembered how busy she can get at work."

_____

_____

_____

- If someone has a feeling or thought you don't understand, ask a clarifying question to try to understand them better; don't guess what they mean. After you've tried it, reflect on the experience. What happened when you practiced asking clarifying questions?

_____

_____

_____

_____

- The next time you're in a situation with someone else that might be sensitive, pause and consider other interpretations of a particular situation, even if the reality of the situation seems obvious to you. Write down any alternative explanations you came up with that did not match your initial appraisal.

_____

_____

_____

_____

- Practice imagining what someone else's experience is like, using empathy—or practice empathy with yourself and assess your own. For example, "I overreacted because I have been disappointed so many times before. This is understandable and I don't need to be hard on myself."

_____

_____

_____

For further reflection, in the spaces below, write down a few times you were successful practicing one of these strategies. What happened? How was it helpful to you in practicing curiosity with yourself and others, and achieving better outcomes in the situations you're in?

What happened? _____

Date: _____

Strategy I used (e.g., reframing, stopping and thinking, challenging yourself, etc.)

_____

What happened? _____

Date: _____

Strategy I used (e.g., reframing, stopping and thinking, challenging yourself, etc.)

_____

What happened? _____

Date: _____

Strategy I used (e.g., reframing, stopping and thinking, challenging yourself, etc.)

_____

What happened? _____

Date: _____

Strategy I used (e.g., reframing, stopping and thinking, challenging yourself, etc.)

_____

Acceptance of Imperfection

Another point I want to highlight about healthy attachments and mentalization is learning to accept imperfection. You might assume here that I'm only speaking to those we might consider as high-strung—people who need to have a perfect home, perfect appearance and so on. For survivors of trauma, flawlessness goes far beyond these stereotypes. Particularly in disruptive home environments, children need to soothe themselves, and this self-comforting often involves a fantasy life in which everything is "just right." Young children in traumatic situations imagine a perfect environment that is safe and embodies a warm and cozy world. Additionally, children who feel a lot of shame can develop an ideal version of themselves to ward off devastating feelings of loss and the idea that they caused others to hurt them. Even as an adult, when you've experienced trauma, you can develop ideas that if you had behaved differently (which often means "better" in some way) you would not have been subject to the random events that have harmed you.

These ideas of perfection involve high standards for ourselves and for others, and this can lead to tremendous difficulty dealing with disappointment when we don't measure up. Again, this is not really about perfection; it's more that disappointment reminds us that there is no ideal world.

In my view, the creation of a supreme internal or external world and the wish for others to be the epitome of good is a way to protect yourself from the reality that the world is full of flawed people who may endanger you. And though this system may seemingly protect you from despair, it often causes more distress. The reality is that none of us are unflawed, and none of us can achieve an ideal world.

If the desire for a perfect world is causing problems for your ability to mentalize and develop secure, healthy relationships with others, practice learning to live with (and potentially embracing) imperfection. Here are some ideas to try.

Sitting with Imperfection

1. Think about the last time you felt you made a mistake. What was it, and how did it make you feel?

   _____

   _____

   _____

   _____

   _____

2. Looking back on it, do you feel you were overly hard on yourself?

   _____

3. When people make mistakes, they can often go between thinking about the infraction all the time (rumination) or not thinking about it at all (evacuation). Have you found yourself in either of these extremes? How can you find ways to distract yourself from thinking about mistakes too much and reflecting on them in a calm, compassionate, and nonjudgmental way?

   _____

   _____

   _____

   _____

4. How could you have soothed yourself? Could you have gotten support and validation from friends, family, or a neutral party, such as a therapist? Perhaps reminded yourself that everyone makes mistakes, or engaged in other soothing self-talk?

_____

_____

_____

_____

5. Think of some ways people typically deal with imperfection. They can compare themselves to others, use humor, and find ways to repair a relationship if that has been involved. Now consider your initial example. What did you do or could have done?

_____

_____

_____

_____

6. Finally, think about the emotions you had after something you regretted. Were you sad, scared, angry with yourself, or upset with someone else? Did past traumas come to mind?

_____

_____

_____

_____

Dealing with imperfection involves accepting the reality of something we have done that is less than ideal without berating ourselves to a point where we can't think about it. Intense feelings about mistakes often have to do with how disappointed and frightened we have been in the past. When things go awry, we can worry that we have been destructive or that something catastrophic will happen. Fortunately, most of the time, our missteps are simply a reminder that we are human. By practicing sitting with and embracing imperfection, we develop more compassion for ourselves and others, and a better ability to develop secure and healthy relationships with them—and with ourselves—to really nourish us.

Conclusion

Mentalization encompasses a variety of concepts that involve metacognition—thinking about how we're thinking—which increases our ability to think in flexible and healthy way, and so makes us more authentic and genuine people. It's linked closely with attachment and our ability to be emotionally attuned to others and ourselves. The important part of mentalization is that it reminds us that we are always a work in progress; knowing ourselves is a key principle when we confront anything that is hard in life. Now that you have some sense of mentalization, you can use these tools in taking the next steps towards healing.

In the next chapter, we'll discuss how avoidance of anything that reminds you of traumatic events you've experienced is a part of life for people with CPTSD, and start a conversation about how much (and if) confronting trauma in a more direct way works for you.

CHAPTER 6

Dealing with Avoidance Mindfully
How to Know When Exposure May Be Helpful

Avoidance is a common symptom of both PTSD and CPTSD, and essentially involves the tendency to circumvent reminders of trauma events. A simple example is someone who was involved in a terrible car accident and afterward avoids being in automobiles. For people who have experienced repeated and multiple traumas throughout their lives, avoidance can be more encompassing, complicated, and confusing. Furthermore, given that some people with trauma histories may not remember all aspects of traumatic events, they may dodge certain thoughts feeling and behaviors without being aware of it.

For example, a client I'll refer to as Martina reported that she noticed that when she was in meetings at work she would often try to sit near the door. She would go to scheduled events sometimes thirty minutes beforehand so she could secure a spot near an exit. When this was not possible, and she could not be near a door or exit, she would have a panic attack. Martina was only vaguely aware of this behavior for a long time. Once she became aware of it, she was still unable to tell me why it happened. It was only after she told me about her experience of having been literally trapped—her parents used to lock her in a dark closet—that we understood this behavior a lot more.

Avoidance involves much more than behaviors, however. Literally any thought or feeling that could be linked to past adverse experiences can be met with attempts to sidestep it. Although sometimes this is conscious, it often is not, as in the example of Martina. Other examples include the urgent need to not listen to a certain song as it may be associated with something difficult, or changing the subject when something activating might be a part of the conversation. However, in PTSD, symptoms of avoidance are fairly straightforward. they involve not thinking about or entertaining ideas of the trauma. But in CPTSD, avoidance can be more complicated, largely because it may operate automatically. It may be less clear which specific thoughts, feelings, or memories are being avoided. Also, it's worth understanding that avoidance can be protective—sometimes in ways you may not necessarily want to change. In the end, the key is to consider the *function* of avoidance in your life and whether that function is adaptive or not: whether it makes it easier for you to live your life, or harder. So, in this chapter, we'll consider how avoidance functions in your life, and how you can intervene if it's not working, using a technique called *exposure*. Exposure can help you make contact with what you've been avoiding, and can be done either on your own or with the help of a qualified therapist.

Before I talk more about how avoidance works—including its benefits and its limitations—let's take a moment to consider how or if avoidance is part of your experience.

Avoidance Symptoms in Complex PTSD

While the universal marker of avoidance is simply attempts to avoid things, like thoughts, behaviors and feelings that can serve as reminders or triggers of traumatic events, it's worth considering the specific ways you might practice avoidance. Below are some symptoms that can be faced by people with PTSD and CPTSD. Check off any of these items that are part of your experience:

- ☐ When thoughts of bad things that have happened to you come into your mind, you try to distract yourself and think of something else.

- ☐ You don't recall much of your childhood and/or significant parts of adulthood.

- ☐ You tend not to recall in detail events in which you may have felt mistreated.

- ☐ You have trouble recalling events in which there was a lot of emotion or fighting.

- ☐ You have feelings of disgust to seemingly benign things in the environment, like songs, soap, cologne, etc., and you don't really understand why.

- ☐ You notice or have gotten feedback that you change the subject suddenly during conversations, and you are unsure why this happens.

- ☐ You try to redirect a conversation when someone asks about you.

- ☐ When other people acknowledge vulnerability, you try to change the subject, or sometimes even get angry.

- ☐ You have strong aversions to certain kinds of people—maybe they remind you of people from your past, or it may not be clear why.

- ☐ You find yourself anxious if you can't sit next to a door or in places where escape might be difficult.

- ☐ You avoid modes of transportation in which you are not in control, like planes, buses, or smaller automobiles that you're not driving.

- ☐ You find that you feel numb much of the time and try to avoid strong emotions.

- ☐ When you have a current crisis, you tend to avoid people who may be available for an authentic discussion about how you are.

- ☐ When someone asks you how you are or brings up something about your life, you redirect and ask about them instead.

These are just a few manifestations of avoidance symptoms that can be experienced. Traumatic experiences are very diverse; to that end, so are the possibilities for circumventing reminders of trauma. However, if you have a lot of things that you find you avoid, keep this in mind, as these are valuable data points you can consider regarding how you (or if you) address avoidance in your recovery.

Note that my view in this chapter is that avoidance is protective, or at least it starts out that way; not all avoidance is bad. I merely want to bring this concept to your attention, and you can decide if the form of avoidance you practice is something that works for you or not. If avoidance ends up not seeming very helpful, we'll consider some ways to address it head on. First, let's think about how avoidance works in more detail.

Avoidance as a Normal Protective Mechanism

Avoidance is a normal consequence of complex trauma and one that I think needs to be respected as something that can protect a person from being overwhelmed. Some researchers and clinicians suggest that avoidance itself can reinforce or strengthen the power of traumatic memories. In other words, the more we avoid, the more our memories can haunt us. This may be true for some traumatic memories—and it may also be true more for those who have PTSD, but not necessarily CPTSD, in which there are more memories to wade through. Also, as I have described in previous chapters, in CPTSD, these memories may be harder to access and may cause more distress when addressed. Recall that emotional regulation—dealing with intense emotions, like the ones that can arise when you recall distressing memories—can be more difficult for people with CPTSD. And so, with avoidance—like any defense related to trauma—it's essential to be thoughtful and mindful about how to deal with this way of coping. I think it's extremely important that avoidance and related ways of dealing with trauma are understood and respected.

Ultimately, my goal in this chapter is to help you figure out a balance between the degree to which you want to engage in avoidance and the degree to which you might want to come into contact with what you once might have avoided, using exposure to particular experiences, sensations, or situations. Exposure therapies encourage you to encounter memories and related thoughts that cause you anxiety, in a controlled setting, so you can deal with the feelings that arise, rather than instinctively reacting to those feelings or continuing to avoid the things that make you anxious.

However, it's important to keep in mind that many therapists believe that talking about trauma at some point is an important part of healing. And in this way, we can consider all therapies in which talking about trauma is an eventual goal to involve a kind of exposure.

Talk Therapies as a Form of Exposure

Historically, many therapists are taught that a key goal is to help trauma survivors develop a *coherent narrative* of their experience. As you experience safety in therapy or in life, most clinicians assume that the next part of healing will involve some aspects of thinking about traumatic events. Although this can be helpful, I'm not sure it always is. People with CPTSD may have had repeated multiple traumas and/or neglect, often starting in early childhood. From a practical standpoint, there may simply be too many traumas to resolve. How would you know where to start? And given the prevalence of severe anxiety and dissociation among some, it may not even be possible to reconstruct many elements of the past. This can make coming up with a narrative difficult.

However, stories are an integral part of human existence. One of the major deprivations that occurs with repeated trauma is that it takes away one's ability to have a tale to tell. Healing, whether it involves therapy or not, can and should help you develop this skill, but it's more realistic that part of the narrative for people with CPTSD involves a loss of coherence—the loss of one's own story. A large number of trauma clients have told me they didn't remember much before high school or even college. It's not clear that these memories *can* come back. For many who have CPTSD, memory has jagged edges and missing pieces. This is a huge loss and can be very painful, but it's a real part of the story for many. And ultimately, you may feel that a non-narrative or a disjointed one feels truer for you than a more "coherent" one.

In fact, whether you're in therapy or trying to heal on your own, what may be most important for you is to create space to be in control of any discussions about trauma. It may be that this is the first time you have felt you have control, and you don't want to risk surrendering that control by diving back into your past; you'd rather continue to build on what you're achieving in the present. Many people are terrified of becoming overstimulated by thinking about terrifying events or even becoming more aware of their thoughts. For example, a client who had been the victim of attempted murder would begin talking about things related to the attack but would become extremely dissociated, which we could describe as "losing himself."

When this happened, we returned to the techniques that worked for him to get these symptoms under control—grounding techniques, creating positive triggers (like engaging in thoughts and activities that resulted in genuine pleasure and positive emotions), mindfulness, and asking his wife to help him—until he felt safe enough to discuss some aspect of what he'd experienced in terms of his trauma background.

With these caveats in mind—that the avoidance you engage in may be helpful for you, and that the common therapeutic approach of having those who've experienced trauma develop a coherent narrative of their own experience is itself a form of exposure, and one you may not want to pursue—let's think more about if exposure therapy may be right for you, and if so, what forms may be helpful. We'll cover some forms of exposure you can do on your own, like expressive writing, and other more complex forms that are often best done with a therapist's help.

What Is Exposure Therapy?

Formal exposure therapies encompass a subset of cognitive behavioral therapy, which is a form of therapy that targets your cognitions or thoughts about yourself and your world, and how those impact your behaviors. There are a number of older and newer therapies that can be considered exposure treatments. Older treatments involve *flooding* and *systematic desensitization*. Flooding is often viewed as a harsher treatment in which people who are frightened of something are encouraged to explore their fears in a fast and dramatic way. An extreme example is if you are afraid of snakes, and your therapist brings a real snake into the office. Systematic desensitization pairs relaxation with slow and gradual visualizations of feared stimuli. It's actually somewhat similar to modern techniques; the general idea of formal exposure is you learn to think of things that are hard but combine this with knowing how to soothe yourself and create a feeling of safety. These therapies have been used for PTSD and also for phobias and specific anxieties. However, flooding in particular is sometimes seen as too harsh to be recommended.

There are two types of newer therapies that are can be considered more formally as exposure for use with people with PTSD and CPTSD. These include *prolonged exposure therapy* and *cognitive processing therapy*. It also includes *eye movement desensitization and reprocessing* (EMDR), although there is some disagreement on EMDR's utility for CPTSD. Below are basic descriptions of these therapies, so you can understand what they are and how they work. After that, I'll guide you to decide which option is right for you: conducting formal exposure with a therapist to bring yourself into contact with things you currently avoid, trying exposure on your own, or not doing exposure at all.

Prolonged exposure therapy teaches individuals to gradually approach their trauma-related memories, feelings, and situations. The goal is to learn that trauma-related memories and cues are not dangerous and do not need to be avoided. Advocates of this approach believe that avoiding reminders of the trauma increases the strength the traumatic event has for you, because fear is reinforced. Exposures are initiated early in treatment with the idea that you can learn that cues and thoughts related to the traumatic event are not inherently dangerous.

Cognitive processing therapy begins with psychoeducation regarding PTSD, thoughts, and emotions. Clients become more aware of the relationship between their thoughts and emotions and begin to identify "automatic thoughts" that may be maintaining PTSD symptoms. Typically, this form of therapy focuses a bit more on cognitions related to traumatic events, and less on the sensations associated with exposure; it also reduces the amount of exposure time clients need to endure, instead guiding them to alter those beliefs related to the trauma that they deem unhelpful to them.

Finally, there's eye movement desensitization reprocessing, or EMDR. It is thought by some to be a kind of exposure therapy, and its efficacy has been found to be comparable to exposure treatments, specifically for PTSD. EMDR involves the client focusing on an image from a traumatic experience they've had while the therapist directs them to engage with certain eye movements, tones, tapping, or other kinds of tactile stimulation. This is said to enhance the processing of the traumatic experience, because the tactile stimulation makes it easier for the client to come into contact with such experiences, and proponents suggest that new neural connections may be made through connecting the traumatic memory with new information (this happens with therapy in general, too).

At their essence, all exposure therapies involve education about the impact of trauma, using techniques to manage emotions both during treatment and when you're recalling difficult events. Exposure therapies can be very helpful, according to research. These treatments are designed to be relatively short-term, and have a great deal of applicability for clients who want fast interventions and/or clients whose finances may be limited. That said, there are limitations to exposure therapies too. It's worth keeping those in mind as you consider which aspects of avoidance you'd like to work on as you continue learning to cope with your CPTSD symptoms.

What Are Limitations of Exposure Therapy?

One downside of exposure therapy is that it can cause a great deal of distress. Hopefully by the time someone tries exposure therapy they already have tools in place to help with the discomfort that results from thinking about traumatic events like the emotion-regulation skills you learned earlier in this book (the ability to know and detect your own emotions as they arise, and the ability to respond to what you feel and think with curiosity and self-compassion). Many clients who have not tolerated exposure treatments found that although it seemed like a good idea to try to tackle some memories of abuse or trauma, they were surprised at how upset they felt.

Without adequate social support, some people can find PTSD/CPTSD symptoms worsen. Unfortunately, I've seen some people have increases in suicidal thinking or have more emotions that feel out of control. However, a savvy therapist using exposure therapy should be able to help clients in these situations by being able to recognize when clients are feeling overwhelmed; if this happens, they should stop the exposure part of the work, and allow space for clients to feel more secure before returning to exposure—if that is what the client wants.

Since exposure therapies require that clients recall distressing events, dropout rates from these formal treatments can be high (up to around 40 percent). Since therapy itself can help people with CPTSD and PTSD, needing to quit therapy is a certainly disappointing outcome. However, it's important to keep in mind that there are many different kinds of therapists and therapies that can help you to deal with trauma. I personally advocate that survivors of trauma should look for clinicians who use a variety of different techniques to help. As you continue your journey to treat CPTSD, you may find that some people you talk to are only interested in using exposure therapy; again, the field of psychology has become somewhat narrow-minded when it comes to the treatment of trauma, and tends to focus on a limited number of techniques, with less emphasis on approaches that utilize several ways to help people. So, while a therapist specializing exclusively in exposure therapy for experiences of trauma can be fine, if that is what you are looking for, keep in mind that there are many approaches to dealing with trauma, and only you get to decide what is best for your own individual journey.

The decision to enter formal exposure therapy is intensely personal, and one that needs to be taken seriously, with great care and consideration. If you are thinking about formal exposure therapy, a good therapist should be able to help you prepare. There are also some factors you can consider on your own.

Is Exposure Right for Me?

Look the following list of items, and check off the ones that describe you.

- ☐ You have specific memories from one or more events that have been traumatic. These events are troubling to you and you would like help in thinking about them.

- ☐ You have some physical distance from the people who have caused you pain and been part of your traumatic experience (e.g., you do not currently live with those you may think about during exposure therapy).

- ☐ Generally speaking, you feel safe and secure in your life now; you are in no actual immediate danger.

- ☐ You have enough emotional support in your life and people to turn to if you suddenly feel worse and need help.

- ☐ You are not burdened with frequent incidences of suicidal ideation or self-harm/self-injury behaviors.

- ☐ You have specific skills and tools in place in the event that you get emotionally overwhelmed.

- ☐ There are specific flashbacks, memories, or nightmares that seem to increase in intensity if you don't think about them.

- ☐ Avoidance behaviors or intrusive thoughts are interfering with your quality of life.

- ☐ You don't use substances excessively as a way to cope with difficult feelings.

If you've checked a lot of items in this list, it may be a sign that you are ready to try formal exposure therapy. If you did not check too many of the previous items, then maybe it's best to wait—and that is okay. Healing from trauma takes many forms, and it's your call on what may be helpful or not.

Trying Exposure Therapy on Your Own: Self-Disclosure

Whether or not you are not ready to try formal exposure therapy with a therapist, you can try some of these techniques on your own to see how they land—and if they feel useful to you—before you see a professional. Formal exposure therapy involves seeing someone who can walk you through some of your difficult memories and experiences or bring you into contact with specific situations and experiences you currently avoid. One way to try some exposure is by remembering that anytime we talk about traumatic experiences, it is a kind of exposure therapy. Thus, if you choose to, you can practice talking with people about your experience on your own.

Note that this can be risky, because yes, disclosure can be hard on you, but also, not everyone can hear about traumatic or difficult experiences. If you decide to share your past with someone, you need to choose wisely—be truly careful and protective of yourself in this way. It can feel like such a devastating blow to think you can trust someone, only to find out that you can't. Let's take a minute to think through your support system for this form of exposure to your trauma experience.

Self-Assessment for Informal Exposure

In psychology, we often say that it's important to have "social support"; it's standard teaching. However, the quality of that social support matters a lot. In fact, research has shown that the wrong kind of support—meaning people who can't listen, people who listen in a superficial way and can only offer platitudes such as "everything happens for a reason", or people who don't spend time trying to find out how you feel—can be detrimental to physical and mental health. So, if you are going to think about who you are going to talk with about your trauma, there are a few things to consider.

1. What kind of support do you want to get? One way I think about answering this is to think about the kind of responses you want. So, when you seek support, do you want someone to respond like Oprah (warm and fuzzy) or Dr. Phil (someone who can give you advice and set you straight)? There is no single right answer, and many different responses can be possible, but try to

think about what works for you and what you want when you are vulnerable with someone.

_____

_____

_____

_____

2. What kind of listening style do you prefer? Are you looking for someone to validate your feelings? Are you wanting someone to say how horrific the event(s) were? Do you want to be reminded of your resilience? Your strength? Should they stay quiet?

_____

_____

_____

_____

3. Remember that, on occasion, natural conversations involve back-and-forth dialogue. If someone wants to share their own traumatic stories or difficult events, would that feel okay and validating, as long as it seems reciprocal (with the other person conveying that they can relate in some way; not, for instance, that they know "exactly how you feel," or that their experience somehow trumps yours)? Or would you prefer someone just listen quietly without remarking, kind of like what happens in 12-step support groups?

_____

_____

_____

_____

4. If you get emotional or start to feel scared, what is the best way you can feel supported? Would you like to be comforted? How? Would you like the other person to put their hand on your shoulder? Give you a hug? Give you space?

    _____

    _____

    _____

    _____

5. If you start to feel dysregulated or worry that you might be feeling out of control, how can the other person help you? Would you like to be reminded of coping skills? Or just a reminder that they're there for you? Or for them to give you space to figure this out for yourself?

    _____

    _____

    _____

    _____

I realize that these questions could seem like a bit of a disappointment from the standpoint that we all wish that people could "just get it right" when we try to talk with them. This understandable ideal is hard to achieve for a few reasons. The first way this can be difficult may have something to do with the nature of trauma survivors. People with CPTSD are incredibly resilient and can be so good at figuring out what people want. And often, their sense is that people want them to be "healthy" or "normal," in ways that sharing something as significant as a trauma experience can challenge. When you decide that you need to be heard, sometimes people can be caught off guard. Remember that you being vulnerable may show a side of yourself that people have not seen before. Sometimes people need time to adjust to the more open version of yourself.

Additionally, we live in an increasingly hyperactive culture. Think of all the images on social media in which people feel pressured to present their lives as happy and enviable. Often on social media, issues related to trauma and other hardships are presented in a one-dimensional way or in a way that does not respect the sheer number or scale of difficulties that you may experience. Further, in a very general sense, authentic conversations regrading vulnerable feelings may seem to take place less and less these days. And of course, people generally often have trouble with conversations that involve vulnerability or things that people have trouble hearing about. Trauma and its realities are often split off and concealed or ignored.

All of this is to say that the previous questions—as awkward as they may be—are an attempt to encourage you to think about what you will need if you decide to talk with people about some of your experiences. We need to protect ourselves and choose our confidants wisely. Often this means considering telling people what we might need before we discuss something hard. And yes, it can feel weird (I get it), but it's better than simply hoping someone will get it right; the truth is, they may not know what you need.

If you opt to use self-disclosure as an exposure strategy, you might take some time to journal about what happened when you tried it, whether those results were "good" or not so good. It can be helpful to give yourself some time and space to debrief. Also be sure to lean on others in your support network or on a therapist or other professional's help if you need it.

Self-Disclosure Self-Debrief

First, after you have tried talking with someone, consider how it went. How did you feel? Did you feel safe, not understood, or confused? Write down the experience here:

_____

_____

_____

_____

_____

Next, consider what you might do differently if it did not go well. Think of things like picking someone else next time, being clearer about what you need, preparing the person for what you want to talk about, or choosing which aspects of trauma you might discuss. This latter point is vital; as trauma survivors, once we start talking about certain things, it can be like opening Pandora's box. By opening up, we then remember more vividly and want to tell multiple stories to someone. It's totally understandable, but once we get on a roll with our memories, we can lose our audience! It's not because people don't care; it's because our experiences can just be a lot. Think about your reactions to this and write about it here:

_____

_____

_____

_____

_____

Finally, if you talked with someone about some aspects of your trauma, think about what worked so you can try to ensure this for the next time:

_____

_____

_____

_____

_____

Trying Exposure Therapy on Your Own: Expressive Writing

Another thing you can do in the absence of professional help is to use expressive writing. This is different from journaling, in that it's designed to be a specific short-term intervention, one that's focused on helping you process particular experiences (though a regular journaling practice is also still very useful for those who enjoy it). And there is extensive research that writing can be very good for you. In terms of expressive writing about trauma, there is data that it helps us emotionally and physically, though it has not been studied in people with CPTSD. The psychologist James Pennebaker is credited with the idea of expressive writing; he's been studying it since the 1980s. Expressive writing can be helpful because it allows you to take a painful experience, identify it as difficult, and make meaning out of it. Translating a tough experience into language causes you to organize your thoughts, and creating a narrative can provide a sense of control.

When it comes to CPTSD, the same caveats described earlier apply. A complete narrative of your traumatic experience may be unavailable to you, and so you may want to be careful to temper your expectations regarding this tool. Nevertheless, it may be worth trying expressive writing as a form of exposure if you have one or two nagging events or experiences that you would like to try to write down so you can think about them further.

Keep in mind that for some people, writing can feel too permanent or real. In other words, sometimes, if we write something down, it can feel too cementing, like something we can't undo or overcome. So, if you decide to try to write about certain memories and events, do so with that in mind.

Ultimately, if you're up for trying expressive writing to start to put together your trauma narrative, here are some rough guidelines:

- Create a space for this special writing and do so when you feel calm and safe. Consider finding time where you can be alone and settle with your thoughts, and maybe have a warm cup of tea with you and/or a cuddly pet or anything else that's comforting.

- Try not to be distracted by your phone or social media. Set aside time, preferably alone if that feels safe. Expressive writing works better with fewer distractions.

- Think about how you want to express yourself. Pen and paper are ideal because it slows you down. You could also write in the note-taking app on a mobile device if that is easier. Research shows recording your voice works well, too.

- Choose a topic. What is bothering you the most?

- Is the topic something you can't talk to anyone else about? If so, this may be a good topic for the privacy expressive writing offers.

- Spelling and grammar don't matter, nor does the quality of your writing. In this medium, no one is watching.

- In that vein, don't share your writing. Try to keep it to yourself, at least initially. If you feel you are writing for an audience, it can change the meaning and authenticity of what you write.

- You can stick with your original topic, but if it leads you to other thoughts and feelings, just go where the writing takes you.

- Sometimes it's helpful to just get some thoughts out, any thoughts, no matter how random they seem. At other times it can be helpful to try to make connections between what you wrote and why it bothers you now. Consider which approach makes sense for you at this moment.

The idea in expressive writing is that it can help us take our thoughts and feelings and translate them into language. This can be helpful because it turns what is in our heads into something more concrete and potentially usable—meaning that we may be able to develop more coping resources in order to deal with our thoughts and feelings related to trauma.

Experts who utilize Dr. Pennebaker's approach say to try it for fifteen to twenty minutes for three to ten days. It may not be a big commitment if you choose wisely and focus on material that isn't overstimulating. That said, keep in mind how you feel and monitor any of your own personal distress signals as you do this. If you feel too overwhelmed, back off and don't feel pressured to resume.

Ultimately, exposure—whether it's through informal means like talking with others or trying to write about it by yourself—is only one way to deal with traumatic events. You can also consider seeing a therapist who can guide you through more detailed recall of events and thoughts and feelings you have avoided. But I hope that I've made it clear throughout this chapter that dealing with your thoughts of trauma and tendency to avoid those ideas are intensely personal decisions, and you can decide for yourself what works for you.

Conclusion

Avoidance is a normal and common adaptive response to trauma, and particularly CPTSD. Although researchers have different opinions on this topic, it may be the case that *not* thinking about some aspects of your background has some utility for you. On the other hand, some people find that confronting certain persistent thoughts or flashbacks through exposure therapy can be helpful. At the end of the day, only you get to decide if you want to confront traumatic or difficult memories. If formal exposure therapy seems like a lot to take on, remember that "exposure" simply means talking and thinking about traumatic events; you can try to do this with people you trust, meaning just trying out talking about your experience. In addition to self-disclosure with trusted people you've vetted, you can also try expressive writing, which has been shown to be helpful for many people with trauma histories, though not as consistently studied among people who have CPTSD.

It's important to remember that you and only you have control over when and how you talk about traumatic memories or anything at all regarding your past. If you try exposure in any therapeutic format and find that it is too overwhelming, remember that you can stop at any time. People with CPTSD need to work to protect themselves from becoming overwhelmed or overstimulated, and there are very good reasons to be protective of yourself, as we will discuss in the next chapter.

CHAPTER 7

Dealing with Suicidal Thoughts and Feelings

One of the more tragic consequences of trauma, maltreatment, and being the victim of random and unfair events is that it can leave survivors beset with thoughts and ideas of suicide and self-destruction. If this is part of your experience, I hope this chapter helps you deal with the intense feelings of helplessness and hopelessness that can lead to thoughts of self-harm, self-injury, or even questions about whether life is worth living. I'll provide skills-based approaches for dealing with these intense feelings, including how to get help if you have a suicidal crisis.

Suicidal Thoughts Are Common

If you've ever thought in even a fleeting way about ending your life, you are not alone. Suicidal thoughts are very common. According to the U.S. Centers for Disease Control (CDC), in 2013 an estimated 9.3 million adults (3.9 percent of the adult U.S. population) reported having suicidal thoughts in the previous year. The percentage of adults having serious thoughts about suicide was highest among adults aged 18 to 25 (7.4 percent), followed by adults aged 26 to 49 (4.0 percent), then by adults aged 50 or older (2.7 percent).

It can be hard to digest how common suicidal ideation can be. The purpose of this chapter is not to overwhelm you, but to let you know you're not alone if you struggle with thoughts of suicide or self-harm and to give you knowledge you can use to deal with what you feel and keep yourself safe.

If suicidal thinking is an issue for you, you likely already know this. But it's still worth considering specific risk factors you might be confronting, so you can figure out what to do about them. So, if it's not too much to do it right now, let's try the following exercise. (It's okay if it's too much right now. The exercise will be there when you're ready.)

Risk Factors for Suicidal Thoughts

If it's not too overwhelming, consider the list of risk factors below, and check off the ones that you feel apply to you. As hard as it is to think about this, it's helpful to know what risk factors to watch for now and in the future.

☐ Severe difficulty sleeping and concentrating

☐ An exaggerated startle response

☐ Anger and agitation

☐ Feeling like a burden to others

☐ Extreme hypervigilance

☐ Anxiety and panic disorder

☐ Severe depression and or bipolar disorder

☐ Medical issues, especially if they're not well treated

☐ Childhood abuse and/or neglect

☐ Chronic pain

☐ Adverse childhood experiences including a parent who was incarcerated, violence between caretakers, someone in the household who was mentally ill or excessively using substances

☐ Difficulty in feeling soothed in the presence of others

☐ History of acting impulsively

☐ The presence of suicidal thinking, especially when there are problems in relationships

☐ Current excessive substance use

☐ Previous suicide attempt

☐ Self-harm or self-injury, such as cutting or restricted eating

☐ Psychotic thinking (thinking that is not based on reality)

☐ Being bullied, particularly if identified as LGBTQ+

☐ Family history of suicide attempts

☐ Feelings of helplessness and hopelessness

It's often hard to think about these issues. But be assured that many people often have feelings or thoughts of death or not wanting to be here. It's just that most people don't act on them. If you have these thoughts, know that like other experiences related to CPTSD, you can consider them data points about how you feel—just as emotions like fear, anger, and anxiety are. And just like those emotions, these thoughts are not things that need to be acted on. However, if you have checked a lot of the above items, consider seeing a therapist to help you deal with what you're thinking and feeling. For readers in the United States, the National Suicide Prevention Lifeline number is 800-273-8255; this number will also take you to the Veterans Crisis line. You can also text the National Crisis line at 741-741. And there are additional avenues for support in the Resources section at the back of this book.

Ultimately, if you are not sure if your situation is serious enough, don't overthink it; ask for help, and get to safety if you are having thoughts that are frightening to you. It's always better to reach out than not.

If you're out of immediate crisis mode, but still struggling with feelings that you're helpless, hopeless, and ashamed, there are strategies that can help. Let's explore some of them now.

Strategies for Managing Self-Destructive Thoughts

The first step to managing self-destructive thoughts is to understand the specific ones you're having. The goal is reducing the impact they have on your day-to-day life and functioning, and keeping yourself from acting on those thoughts in destructive ways.

Trauma survivors can be more prone to thoughts of death and suicide. Although we don't understand all the reasons why this is, trauma makes us feel helpless, hopeless, and ashamed, all of which can cause us to excessively devalue ourselves and our worth. Also, for those who have had aggressive parents who may have at times struggled in the role of being a parent, as kids we sense that; and a person who had such a parent may become suicidal during periods in which they feel that they may be "too much" for others. The idea of being a burden is something talked about often by people who have been or are suicidal. Feeling this way can be a major trigger.

A slightly less dire idea comes from decades of anecdotal clinical experience about suicidal thinking. As the sociologist and psychotherapist Lillian Rubin powerfully describes in her 2001 memoir, *Tangled Lives,* the idea is that some people who have difficult life experiences (particularly in childhood) keep the idea of suicide in their minds as a kind of emergency exit. The thinking goes something like this: *Things are really bad and I feel trapped. However, if I can't stand it any longer, I can always leave; I can escape.* If we look at it this way, we can conclude that suicidal thoughts are sometimes a paradoxical way people keep themselves going. That mode of thinking can persist even when the situation that first led a person to think this way is long over.

There are many ways suicidal thinking and thoughts of death can impact people. In fact, suicidal ideations exist on a kind of spectrum, from passive thoughts to self-destructive actions, which can look something like this.

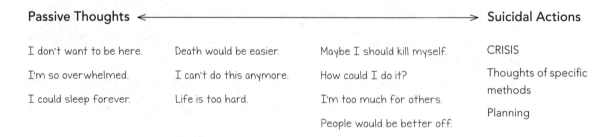

Passive Thoughts ⟵⎯⎯⎯⎯⎯⎯⎯⎯⎯⎯⎯⎯⎯⎯⎯⎯⎯⎯⟶ **Suicidal Actions**

I don't want to be here.	Death would be easier.	Maybe I should kill myself.	CRISIS
I'm so overwhelmed.	I can't do this anymore.	How could I do it?	Thoughts of specific methods
I could sleep forever.	Life is too hard.	I'm too much for others.	Planning
		People would be better off.	

Here's a drastic question, but one that's worth considering: Do you currently consider yourself somewhere along this spectrum? Whether you're in crisis or your self-destructive thoughts are more passive and occasional, it's worth learning coping strategies that can help you deal with them.

What Your Thoughts Might Mean About Your Relationships

Whether they're active or passive, suicidal thoughts are something we need to pay attention to, in order to avoid them becoming overwhelming or feeling like we need to act on them. What's more, suicidal thoughts, especially when they're passive or mild, also give us a good opportunity to understand if what we're feeling may be related to difficulties we're having in certain relationships—for instance, a sense we're being judged by someone we know and love, or needs we have that aren't being met. Below I'll provide some journaling exercises regarding the possible meaning of these thoughts, and after that I'll suggest some specific coping skills.

Often, suicidal thoughts can creep up in the context of relationships. It does not mean that others have done something wrong, exactly, but may be a kind of automatic response when you sense certain thoughts of feelings from others. Consider the last time you felt suicidal. Write down what you remember:

_____

_____

_____

_____

_____

Who was the last person you were with before feeling this way? Was there anything weird or off about the interaction?

_____

_____

_____

Looking back, did you sense any aggression or anger, even irritation? Was it in you, the other person, or both?

_____

_____

_____

Were you worried someone else may have been exhausted by you, perhaps felt you were "too much"?

_____

Did you worry that someone was envious of you?

_____

Were you troubled by wanting something more from someone in your life?

_____

Did you worry that whatever feelings were present—in you or the other person—could lead to the ending of that relationship?

_____

These are difficult topics to consider, but since we are evolved to be relational beings, our close connections can be important triggers for suicidal thoughts. If you described feeling suicidal in response to any of the above situations, it's important information to have. It means that you can get triggered in the context of your relationships—and it may mean you need to protect yourself from certain people, perhaps by being more assertive and setting limits with them. It may also mean that you could work on not taking things as personally. People who care about us can get frustrated with us for a variety of reasons. Sometimes their reactions are not about us at all. Sometimes they might be triggered by us, but their reactions may be outsized in proportion to the situation or influenced by experiences they've had that have nothing to do with us.

But often, especially if we are not secure in our own identities and are perhaps worried about the impact of our own intense emotions in ourselves or others, we can then get worried that we're too much for the people around us. Depending on the level or trauma we have experienced, we can move slowly or quickly to thoughts that others may be better without us. These kinds of faulty thoughts need to be challenged. First, remember that every single person I have ever met who has had suicidal thoughts has people (and often, pets) that need them to continue to be around. Second, whatever ideas of low self-worth that can lead people to feel suicidal are *never* realistic. People who feel suicidal are *unrealistically hard on themselves.*

If this feels like something you struggle with, coping will involve both behavioral and cognitive strategies. First, we'll focus on cognitions: the need to push back against negative thoughts about your own self-worth. This is where mindfulness—the capacity to consider our own internal experience nonjudgmentally—can be very useful. It allows us to understand that thoughts simply contain data we can consider, and they are not mandates for how we should act.

Combatting Suicidal Thoughts

Which suicidal thoughts *related to self-worth* (judgments about how much or little you matter) do you tend to struggle with? Write them down here.

_____

_____

_____

_____

_____

Even if suicidal thoughts are a constant part of your emotional life, it's worth thinking about how to quiet these thoughts in a compassionate way—and how to find ways to meet the needs that these thoughts—painful though they may be—might signify.

Some general ideas for coping with suicidal thoughts:

- Consider this fact: All 29 people who survived their suicide attempts off San Francisco's Golden Gate Bridge have said they regretted their decision as soon as they jumped.

- Consider the mantra: Suicide is a permanent solution to what is often a temporary problem.

- Use mindfulness to remember that suicidal thoughts are just thoughts that should be accepted and understood for what they are—the impressions of a moment and not commands we need to follow. Also, use mindfulness to keep in mind that thoughts are potentially changeable.

  Here's a brief mindfulness exercise you can try: *Settle into a comfortable position. Take a breath and focus on breathing into your belly, letting it expand as your inhale. As you exhale, just notice any sensations in your body. Notice what areas feel tense and what areas feel relaxed. Don't judge the sensations. As you get more into your body, you may notice uncomfortable emotions. Remember that emotions are a part of life, serve as valuable information that can guide us and we can endure them and even keep them under control.*

- Use the grounding techniques described in chapter 4.

- Distraction can be a great tool. Distraction includes anything you do to get your mind to another place—including meditation, if that works for you, or hobbies, exercise, computer or virtual games, work, or anything else that takes you away from the suicidal thoughts and immerses you in another task or project. If social media is a distraction, that's great! If it makes you feel worse, though, don't engage until you are feeling better.

- Movement of any kind is helpful when you're struggling with suicidal thoughts, but vigorous exercise is an especially powerful antidepressant/distraction.

- If you have a thought of something from your past that is distressing, tell yourself: *I don't have to think about that situation now.* Avoid going down rabbit holes involving hard memories, unless you are with someone with whom you feel safe.

- Talk to yourself regarding suicidal thoughts. Push back on them by saying: *I don't feel this way all the time. This is a temporary glitch in my brain and it means I need to take better care of myself.*

- Make sure you are getting enough restorative sleep. It's an essential element to caring for yourself and feeling well.

- Data on this is still emerging, but consider your diet—limit processed foods and sugar and increase intake of fruits, vegetables, and fiber. Diet is another lifestyle factor that can potentially exacerbate low moods and make them worse.

- Thoughts of death or dying can be an indicator you are not getting something you need. Consider finding ways to feel more whole and satisfied in all aspects of life.

If suicidal thoughts seem connected to relationships, consider the following strategies:

- Practice stating what you need, without guilt.

- Maybe consider leaning on someone less if they seem like they need space.

- Widen your social support network so you have more people around to help you meet your emotional needs; this way, you can put less burden on relationships that might be buckling under the pressure you're inadvertently putting on them.

- If you feel guilty about needing too much, remember this may be about the past, rather than a realistic assessment of the situation you're in now.

- Find people who can share your struggles of feeling suicidal: build relationships, through support groups or similar venues, in which you can share your struggles honestly.

Yes, it's awful to have these thoughts, but it's important to challenge them with compassion for yourself. Get help if needed so that those thoughts do not lead to actions.

The Trauma of a Suicidal Crisis

There's a difference between passive suicidal thoughts—which can be a common part of life, especially for those who've experienced trauma—and serious suicidal thoughts that lead to a crisis. And while it's a heavy topic of conversation, it's worth taking a closer look at what an active suicidal crisis can look like, so you're prepared to cope with any discomforts you might be facing in the future—and able to recover from what can, ultimately, be a trauma itself.

Yes, a suicide attempt or serious suicidal thinking (ideation) are *both* traumatic events. It's truly terrifying, and genuinely something that people do not understand unless they have been through it. People I've known who have been close to ending their lives also experience the terror that they could feel that way again. We don't know enough about the intensely personal and agonizing thinking that takes over when people come close to trying to end their life. What we do know is that in a lot of cases, a person's thinking changes in a significant way. And in the end, I think of suicide attempts—or even seriously suicidal thinking—as a form of trauma that becomes layered among previous traumas. Consider the following example:

> *Rachel was in her fifties when her partner of fifteen years left her for a younger woman at her workplace. Rachel was devastated and became increasingly suicidal. By the time she took an overdose of pills, she felt taken over by what is often described as a suicidal trance or suicidal mode. For weeks, suicide was the only thing on her mind. She imagined taking her own life continually and rehearsed the scene in her mind over and over. She also heard voices telling her that she was worthless and should die. She had never had this latter experience before and it was utterly terrifying. She barely remembered anything about her suicide attempt, only the sense of horror and confusion after she woke up in the hospital. At that point, she was not suicidal and not even sure how or why she had come to be feeling that way in the first place.*

One of the more frightening things about a suicidal trance or mode is that a kind of thinking takes over that feels foreign. These thoughts can be like an invasion in which people forget reasons to live. And the fact that one's mind can betray them in such a way is a true hallmark of the terror and trauma of a suicidal crisis.

Ultimately, trauma results in confusion about our own power. Whether it's trauma we experienced in childhood or as an adult, some traumas result in people feeling more powerful than they actually are—that is, feeling like they have more ability to influence situations or outcomes than they actually have. They believe that they are responsible for the fact that they were injured, that the hurts inflicted on them were the result of something they did or did not do. When someone is seriously considering suicide or has made a suicide attempt, similar ideas of their own power and control become terrifyingly real.

People with histories of multiple and chronic traumas likely felt that their lives were endangered at some point, either through the reality of a situation involving violence or through the intensity of the emotions they've felt, which can feel so strong as to overwhelm and overtake their lives. To have this sense of danger felt internally—to feel as though they themselves could put their own lives in jeopardy—is another cruel and terrifying facet of life and the aftermath of trauma. One client talked with me about this and expressed it very plainly. He said, "I don't want to kill myself now. But it's weird, you know? I could. I could simply choose to die at any time." This is a reality that most people try to distance themselves from, but it is true. It seems that once someone has come close to suicide, it changes them. It makes the idea of death seem ever-present and ever-possible. And this experience becomes a part of the trauma story, spoken or unspoken.

If you have been in this situation, it's important to name the traumatic nature of a suicidal crisis and express compassion for yourself. I'd urge you to find people who can relate, through a support group or something similar. While well-meaning people like your loved ones may want to you to move past suicidality and focus on living, thinking and talking about the meaning of suicidal thoughts, actions, and their consequences can be very helpful. This is usually done a while after having been acutely suicidal. It's part of making meaning of such a confusing and frightening event.

It's also important to learn skills that will prepare you for any suicidal crisis you might experience in the future. The reality is that though few of us expect to be in this position—and my earnest hope for you is that you are never are—it's better to be informed if it happens. So, let's begin by looking at the warning signs of a crisis, and the differences between occasional thoughts of suicide and an active suicidal crisis or suicidal mode or trance.

Understanding the Risks of a Suicidal Crisis

Consider the following list of risk factors for suicidal crisis, checking off any items that apply to you or your life right now. You can come back to this list anytime in the future that you feel yourself approaching a point of crisis; it can help make sense of what you're going through and what you're feeling and thinking, which in turn can determine how you can help yourself and give yourself what you need.

☐ Stressful life events such as a relationship loss, job loss, severe financial strain

☐ Recent loss of someone you know from suicide

☐ Withdrawal from people who have been supportive

☐ Constant thoughts of death and dying

☐ Giving away possessions

☐ A feeling that there is no other way out

☐ A feeling that you are an excessive burden on others

☐ A feeling that not being here is the only thing that could feel better

☐ Rehearsing the scene of ending life over and over

☐ Excessive planning around the idea of ending life

☐ A feeling that others would be better off if you were not here

☐ Extreme feelings of hopelessness and helplessness

☐ An extreme sense of oneself as being toxic or even poisonous

☐ Feeling that your thoughts are out of control

☐ Severe sleep disturbance

☐ Having a serious medical problem, especially if it involves pain

It may be very hard to go through these risk factors, but if you have checked a lot of these items, it's a sign that you should seek help from a mental health professional as soon as you can. There is a big difference between suicidal thoughts and the development of severe suicidal thinking, or what is known as a suicidal trance or suicidal mode. It's vital to catch yourself before you get to the point of suicidal thoughts taking over. Once this happens, it's harder to get help.

What to Do If You Are Suicidal

If you are seriously suicidal or even struggling with thoughts of suicide that you are not intending to act on, please consider getting a therapist. If you have a therapist, be sure to talk about your thoughts related to death in general, whether or not that involves taking matters into your own hands. Ideally, therapists should ask frequently about suicidal thoughts, but some just don't do this—especially once someone has been in therapy for a while. So, while it may not be ideal, it's important that you take charge of your mental health in this situation. Bring up these thoughts when they occur.

As you likely already know, if you are seriously considering suicide, you should act in a way that gets you to safety. If the risk is immediate, call 911 or have someone take you to the emergency room of the closest hospital. Additionally, in the United States you can call the National Suicide Prevention Lifeline at 800-273-8255, or you can also text 741-741. If you are not sure your situation is serious enough, don't overthink it. Ask for help and get to safety if you are having thoughts that are frightening to you.

Outside of an immediate crisis, it's important to have people to talk with if you are prone to suicidal thinking. This can be therapist, a group, or even friends or partners who are aware of your potential suicidality. Often, a therapist will develop what is known as a crisis plan with clients. This plan is a way to cope with immediate and acute issues like suicide. But if you're not seeing a therapist, you can do it on your own or with someone you trust, and we're going to develop one now.

The idea of a crisis response plan is to create something that you can carry with you so that you know what to do if you get into a suicidal crisis. Craig J. Bryan (executive director of the National Center for Veterans Studies) developed the following guidelines for crisis response planning (I've modified the guidelines slightly here):

Crisis Response Plan (CRP)

These guidelines were written as something that a therapist and client do together. We're about to develop your own here, but do keep in mind that preparing a plan with a therapist or someone else you trust could be more impactful. That said, let's try it out.

Crisis Response Plan

1. Understand the rationale: Once a person becomes suicidal, it can be hard to remember how to access coping resources. Therefore, complete a safety plan before a suicidal crisis if you can. That way, you'll have all your resources in place, thought about when you were in a calmer state of mind.

2. What are your personal warning signs of a suicidal crisis? Some common signs are getting more depressed, noticing a change in your thinking, feeling darker, heavier, more tired, more agitated, arguing with people more, and thinking of death. Write down any thoughts that may accompany this state of mind, like if you find yourself thinking, "Things will never get better," or similar.

    _____

    _____

    _____

    _____

    _____

3. Write down the self-management/coping strategies you can use in this situation. Consider any hobbies that make you feel grounded, exercise and movement, getting outside, uplifting music, playing games on your phone, drinking a cup of coffee or tea, going for a walk, and safe things that can offer distractions.

    _____

    _____

    _____

    _____

4. Identify reasons for living. Consider people in your life who depend on you, your partner, pets, friends, children, people in your religious group, or where you work or volunteer. Think of things that bring you pleasure or joy. Think of your values and what makes life meaningful. (Remember that if you become suicidal it may be hard to recall these things, so be sure they are highlighted on your app or index card, once you transfer your plan there.)

    _____

    _____

    _____

    _____

    _____

5. Identify social supports. Who can you lean on when you are in distress, or even if you are worried you may get distressed? Think about people who make you feel safe, who can offer distractions and who have been there for you in the past. This can include current mental health clinicians as well.

    _____

    _____

    _____

    _____

6. If you're in crisis, who can you call and what can you do? Perhaps it's a person who can and will answer the phone and show up for you, such as a partner, close friend, or family member—someone who can talk to you and help you think about going to the hospital or seek other intervention. Write down those phone numbers and the National Suicide Prevention Lifeline or other hotlines. Identify the best institutions in your area to go to if you do have a crisis—which hospitals have a good mental health emergency program, and which take your insurance, for example—and the people in your life the staff should call. Write

down those places and the steps you will take to get there if you feel like you want to hurt yourself or try to end your life. Last, call 911 if there is an emergency, and use your plan to help inform the emergency responders.

_____

_____

_____

_____

_____

7. Finally, review the plan, ideally with a trusted person, and think about how likely it will be used in the event of a suicidal crisis. Transfer it to an index card or an app, if you prefer. (One popular app is Safety Plan, which has similar instructions as those recommended above. Other apps include notOK and BeSafe. Keep in mind that while you can carry a plan on your smartphone, from a simple behavioral conditioning perspective, smartphones are associated with anxiety—social media alerts, email alerts, and texts: all things that could cause stress, in a crisis situation, that a simple index card may not.) Rewrite it for clarity if you need to.

Having access to a plan that you carry with you at all times can help you navigate a crisis and, equally as important, access the part of you that wants to live. When in the storm of a suicidal crisis it can be hard to remember what you need to do, even if that seems obvious when you are feeling well. For example, I was recently with one client who tends to find the winter months unbearable and had a previous suicide attempt that season. As we were heading in to the colder and darker months, I suggested we create a safety plan, even though she was not currently suicidal. She remarked while we were doing it that it was soothing to think about this aspect of herself while in a non-suicidal state, that it made her feel safe. She also told me that talking about this aspect of herself made her feel seen by me, as she had not previously felt like she could talk about these most private and disquieting aspects of her experience.

Finding Meaningful Support Around Suicidal Thoughts

Struggling with suicidal thoughts and feelings is often a part of surviving trauma. And it's one of the hardest things to talk about and endure. If you've been in this situation, it's crucial to find people you can talk with. Although suicidal thoughts can be intensely personal and private, and some people think about suicide every day, when you talk about it, it really does help. Unfortunately, many people who have felt suicidal have a hard time finding people with whom they can have meaningful discussions about this. In fact, in one study that talked with over 300 people who had been suicidal, a majority felt strongly that stigma against suicidal thoughts made it hard for them to even talk with therapists. Therefore, it's vital that you find people and create a support network—whether professionals or not—who can get where you are coming from and support you without judgment.

Strengthening Your Social Support

Think about the people closest to you. Make a list of those who come to mind right away.

Then, on a scale of 1 to 5, rate your comfort level of talking with them if you feel suicidal or have suicidal thoughts. A score of 1 indicates you'd feel very unlikely to talk to this person and 5 is very likely comfortable.

1	2	3	4	5
Very Unlikely		Very Likely		Comfortable

	1	2	3	4	5
	1	2	3	4	5
	1	2	3	4	5
	1	2	3	4	5
	1	2	3	4	5

Thinking about your responses, are there things you can do that might make you feel more comfortable in talking with the above people about suicidal thoughts? One way to think about this is to consider that people close to you may not know or understand the depths of your despair at times. Can you talk with them about this when you are not in crisis? Could you say to them something like, "At times, I can feel so low that I have thoughts about hurting myself. Is that something we could talk about if I get to that place?" What ideas come to mind?

_____

_____

_____

_____

Now, let's think outside of your usual support. People often forget who could be really there for them; the truth is, sometime people who are not as close to us as our closest kin and friends can be the most helpful in a crisis. In fact, I have talked with a number of people who don't even consider putting their spouses at the top of their support list. This is fine. Think about people who might be more casual acquaintances or whom you don't see often—maybe old college or work friends, maybe a spiritual leader or someone from your religious affiliation, maybe an old mentor, or a distant family member—who could be there for you if you need to talk or even need a distraction.

_____

_____

_____

_____

Finally, consider new relationship options. As we get older, it's much harder to make friends, but think about ways you can either find new people to relate to or deepen relationships you already have. This could look like going to lunch with an acquaintance, setting up a play date with that parent you always run into, or even asking the person you see a few times a week at the coffee shop if they want to have lunch with you. What are some ways you might find different friends?

_____

_____

_____

_____

Widening this network is important because when we are feeling good, we often don't think as much about our existing social support system. Think of it like planning for a rainy day; when the sun is out you don't need the same things as when there is a storm forecast. You may not need that umbrella or those galoshes by the time you get home, but it is good to know you had them on call. Plus, let's be honest. It's hard to find people who can be a good friend *all* of the time. No one person can do it all for us. The more people we have around, the better.

Conclusion

Suicidal thoughts and feelings are the devastating legacy of trauma. These thoughts may be a part of life; and they may lead to a crisis in which you're not sure life is worth living. Like many things related to trauma, it's not fair you have been through what you have, and the consequences are equally unjust. Coping with this involves knowing the risks of suicidal thinking or actions, making a crisis response plan, and finding the right kind of support. You can harness your own internal resources as well.

Suicide can sometimes feel like giving into those who have harmed us or harbored negative thoughts about us. But when all seems hopeless, recall the quote attributed to George Herbert: "Living well is the best revenge." You *can* live well after surviving trauma and you can do so without needing to punish yourself. When you struggle with suicidal or self-defeating thoughts, they can be a part of your life, but they do not have to own your life.

CHAPTER 8

When Substance Use Becomes a Problem

Sabrina, who was 26 and just starting law school, said she was coming to therapy because of anxiety. She was from the Midwest, with parents she described as "very liberal," one of whom was a daily and heavy drinker and the other who used to "smoke weed" with her many siblings. Sabrina was never involved in these activities, which mirrored her feelings about her childhood. Her older sisters were viewed as much more interesting and got a lot more attention from her parents. Furthermore, Sabrina was often treated to a host of complaints about everything from her looks to her level of intelligence, especially when her parents were using. She told me later in her therapy that she realized from very young age that she was "born into the wrong family." She was isolated throughout much of high school and described herself as "mostly out of it," but when she relocated for college, she lived in the dorm and met many people who were enthusiasts of using substances of all kinds. Sabrina favored party drugs such as MDMA (ecstasy or molly), and she found she could also drink a lot of hard liquor. She also found that at times she was in danger with people who did not respect her boundaries, in a way her level of intoxication made it hard to deal with. Despite this, over the course of college she found beer and marijuana to be soothing and began using these daily. When I asked Sabrina if her substance use bothered her, she wasn't entirely sure, but she was able to talk about how alcohol and pot kept her from thinking "bad thoughts." Yet, I wondered— and I think she did too—if law school might make it difficult for her to keep up with her use. This eventually became something she wanted to think about in her therapy.

People have long used substances for pleasure, self-medication, or experimentation. Substance use is also common among survivors of trauma and complex trauma, for any number of reasons. The issue of substance use is also a complicated one, with users risking inherent judgment for their choices—judgment that can sometimes ignore the contexts in which they use. As a clinician, I respect people's needs or interests in using substances of all kinds—and so, in this chapter, I'll work with you to take a curious and neutral stance on substance use: a stance that's more interested in how your use of substances functions in your life and not whether it's "good" or "bad." We'll think about how you view your substance use, and whether you consider it a problem or an obstacle to functioning.

If you use substances as a way to deal with trauma-related symptoms, know that many other people do too, but this can also cause a great deal of shame. Further, excessive use of drugs and alcohol can be a factor influencing further victimization, as being intoxicated can make us more vulnerable (though this is *not* to say that people who are intoxicated are responsible for their victimization). This highlights the need for compassion and sensitivity when thinking about the matter of substance use.

Substance use is complicated and difficult to treat for both psychological and neurological reasons. Many reward centers in the brain are triggered when we use certain substances. Additionally, substances can sometimes seem to make it easier to deal with emotions. Stimulating drugs promote activation and distraction; sedating drugs can quiet the mind. And many substances can make social interactions easier. Since people with CPTSD are often constantly at risk of being overwhelmed by thoughts and feelings, my view is we need to treat substance use like any other symptom—which is to say, you're allowed to decide how best to address it given how it functions in your life. What do you want to do about your use, if anything? Keep in mind the answer to this question is *your* call to make; my role here is as a guide, not a judge or jury, and I aim to provide you the information you'll need to make the choice that's best for you.

Before we think more about your relationship to substances, let's think a bit more about how common it is to overuse and/or self-medicate with substances.

The Increase in Problematic Substance Use

We are living in a time of extreme use of drugs and alcohol and deaths of despair, which are related. In 2019, public health professionals Steven Woolf and Heidi Schoomaker published an article analyzing life expectancy data collected by the CDC and all-cause mortality rates listed in the US Mortality Database from 1959 to 2017. They noted that although life expectancy had been steadily rising, it decreased after 2014 related to an increase in mortality from specific causes (drug overdose, suicides, organ system diseases) among young- and middle-aged adults of all racial groups, with an onset as early as the 1990s and with the largest relative increases occurring in the Ohio Valley and New England. In many places in the United States, midlife mortality increased, caused by drug overdoses, alcohol abuse, suicides, and a diverse list of diseases related to substance use. Of course, it makes sense to partially blame the opioid epidemic, which has been plaguing the United States and Canada for a number of years. However, while substance abuse and dependency are complicated, there is strong evidence that these afflictions can often be linked with trauma histories, PTSD, and CPTSD.

Links Between Trauma and Substance Use

Up to 65 percent of people with PTSD (as distinct from CPTSD specifically) have been found to also have a substance use disorder. A study in 2019 found that a provisional PTSD diagnosis nearly doubled the risk of nonfatal overdose among people who used illicit drugs, including opiates. About 30 percent of people with PTSD have alcohol dependence; they are more likely to have experienced childhood adversity and a higher likelihood of using substances to relieve PTSD symptoms. Among individuals with PTSD, heavy alcohol use is associated with a greater number of and more severe PTSD symptoms, suggesting that substance use can be used to self-medicate PTSD symptoms.

Trauma is a risk factor for substance abuse, and substance abuse is also a risk factor for trauma. For example, among people who were dependent on cocaine and seeking treatment, the most common adult traumatic events people experienced were witnessing someone's death or serious injury, dealing with a natural disaster, physical assault, accident, and/or sexual assault. One negative thing about using too many substances is it can make us more vulnerable to being used or exploited—or even ending up in the wrong place at the wrong time.

Whether the substance use of a person who's been through trauma is a problem should be determined by the person themselves and input from their loved ones. But there are some factors you can look to when you're trying to determine if your substance use is a problem for you. We'll use the self-medication hypothesis, a helpful and compassionate way to understand problematic substance use. Let's begin by thinking about your relationship with substances.

Factors that Indicate Problems with Use of Substances

☐ You can't go a day without your preferred substance.

☐ Using your substance has interfered with your life in terms of work, relation-ships, or childcare.

☐ You think about your preferred substance much of the time—how you will get it, imagining what it will be like.

☐ You have endangered yourself or taken excessive risks in getting the substance.

☐ You change as soon as you have your substance (e.g., you are different after just one drink).

☐ You engage in risk-taking behaviors after a small amount of alcohol or drugs.

☐ Using drugs or alcohol makes you less available for people who care about you.

☐ You have tried to stop using many times, but it has not worked.

☐ People close to you have told you that the way you drink or use drugs is hurtful/alienating to them.

☐ You binge drink, meaning you have at least four or five drinks in the span of about two hours.

☐ You get angry at others who ask about your use of substances.

☐ You have used alcohol or drugs to the point that others have wondered if you are conscious or had to call 911.

☐ You have used alcohol or drugs to the point of blacking out and not remem-bering what has happened. (For instance, waking up in your bed and not remembering how you got there.)

☐ You engage in risk-taking behaviors when using drugs or alcohol, such as unsafe sex, stealing, or hanging out with people who may not have your best interest in mind.

☐ You can't be around people who won't drink or do drugs like you do.

☐ You have had alcohol or drugs in the mornings to deal with a hangover.

☐ You feel guilty about your use of substances.

☐ Using feels like a familiar friendship you can't part from.

☐ When using, you engage in aggressive behaviors.

☐ You have been told you have medical problems as a result of using substances (e.g., heart problems or worrisome liver-function tests).

☐ You've driven and/or gone to work while still under the influence of the substance.

☐ You've had negative consequences as a result of using substances (like a DUI, problems at work, friends leaving), but they have not changed your use.

If you have checked a lot of the items above, consider that your relationship with substances may be something you want to think about and address. And even if you haven't checked many items, the ones you have checked might signal aspects of your substance abuse or your life that you want to handle differently. The hopeful news is that there are a number of ways to deal with problematic substance use. As a start, let's consider how your current substance use might function as a form of self-medication. To be clear, substance use is often not a great long-term solution to chronic problems, but if your relationship with substances has become harmful, it's helpful to understand *why* you might be drawn to using (or perhaps overusing) substances so you can intervene.

When Substance Use Is Self-Medication

Some people use drugs or alcohol as a way to self-medicate. The most obvious example of this is drinking to quiet intrusive memories or flashbacks. In 1997, Harvard professor Edward Khantzian introduced the self-medication hypothesis of substance use, an idea that is now familiar to many:

Traumatized individuals with limited capacities to psychologically dissociate may attempt to produce similar soothing or numbing effects by using psychoactive substances… These substances are used to enter and maintain dissociative-like states.

In other words, drugs and alcohol can help a person dissociate, which as we've already noted, is a way of coping with trauma that many people with CPTSD experience even without substances. As I noted in chapter 4, dissociation is an escape when there feels like there is no other escape. It makes sense that a person with trauma would engage in substance use in this manner.

As with dissociation, substance use can sometimes get people away from flashbacks and intense feelings that feel scary or negative. Sexual assault survivors with PTSD—who believed that substance use would reduce their distress—were more likely to have problematic alcohol use. Additionally, several studies have suggested that people with substance use problems without PTSD tend to relapse in *tempting* situations, whereas people with PTSD and substance use disorder report using substances in response to *negative* situations.

Before I talk about specific ways to deal with what you might consider problematic substance use, let's do something that might be unexpected. Let's take a moment to consider meanings, including what is useful about using your preferred substance(s).

Making Meaning of Your Substance Use

Just taking a moment to think about how much alcohol and drugs you take, do you feel it is too much? Circle one:

Yes   No   I don't know

Has taking substances started to feel out of control for you? If so, when did this start?

_____

_____

If using has become automatic for you, try to remember when it wasn't. Were there any triggers for taking substances?

_____

_____

_____

Thinking deeper, were there thoughts or feelings which you wanted to get rid of by taking substances?

_____

_____

_____

Does taking substances seem to help you deal with anxiety or depression?

_____

Now just take some time and think about what you enjoy about using. Think as specifically as possible. For example, do substances quiet your mind, activate you, make you feel more in control, easier to do certain things? Write down anything that comes to mind.

_____

_____

_____

_____

What are the negative consequences you've experienced from using?

_____

_____

_____

_____

If you could change anything about the way you use alcohol or drugs, what would it be? Would you want to stop completely? Use in moderation or only on certain days and times, like a family holiday?

_____

_____

_____

_____

I think it's useful for people to discuss what may be helpful about their substance use for two reasons. First, people who excessively use substances often hear repeatedly and judgmentally that they should stop, with the implication that the behavior of taking substances is all bad. Though this message might be well-intentioned, it's often not helpful for someone with an intense relationship to substances. Second, people often feel substances can do something for them; for some people with CPTSD and PTSD, use can seem soothing. So, it's important to notice, understand, and think about the meaning of substances in your life—these are data points that can inform your trauma recovery. It's especially helpful to do this without judgment and in a neutral way.

It's also true that after some time, taking substances can become or seem automatic, and lead to addiction. Indeed, substance use is also thought to particularly impact people who have biological/genetic vulnerabilities to addiction. In this case, it's a bit harder to think about the meaning of substance use. And though it does not happen for everyone, what starts out as self-medication can lead to something that spins out of control. There are also health risks to overusing drugs and alcohol. As I said when starting this chapter, I do not want to be judgmental; substance use is personal, and only you get to decide if it interferes with your life. But when using becomes extensive, it can interfere with your healing; it can cause problems with reclaiming your identity and continuing to develop a relationship with your own mind.

In the next section, we'll talk about ways to gain more control over your use of substances if this is something you want to do.

On Your Own: Treatment Options for Substance Use

Treatment options you can take on your own include pursuing 12-step programs like Alcoholics Anonymous or Narcotics Anonymous, and harm reduction, or the practice of using incremental steps to moderate your use so it's less of a problem for you.

Twelve-Step Programs

Twelve-step programs were adapted from the guidelines set by the 1939 book *Alcoholics Anonymous*. The "Big Book," as it is affectionately called by proponents, lent its name to the support group now known as Alcoholics Anonymous (AA). There are now dozens of 12-step groups that help "addicts" (this term is part of 12-step culture), involving everything from drugs and alcohol to gambling, food, sex, and even workaholism. It's an abstinence model of treatment, meaning the goal is to refrain from any substance or behavior that's deemed an addiction. Groups are peer led and use a sponsor system that encourages or requires a senior person in the program to offer support and mentoring. For example, one person I work with in one of the food addiction–related programs speaks with a sponsor every day. Their conversations are not just related to food; they often sound like mini-counseling sessions. However, different 12-step programs have different levels of flexibility regarding sponsor contact. The other unique thing about 12-step programs is that they are global and relatively consistent. People can find an AA meeting in many parts of the world. Each group has a different culture, and participants are encouraged to find meetings that seem like a good fit.

Critics of 12-step programs suggest that it is a model rooted in white maleness that encourages the belief in a monotheistic god. For example, the concept of "surrendering to a higher power" is involved in 12-step work. This way of thinking is not for everyone; it certainly does not always provide a warm home for atheists (though there are specific 12-step groups for people of differing beliefs, including atheism). Yet, it's also true that spirituality and religiosity are associated with better coping while involved in 12-step programs. In general, though, empirical support for 12-step programs is widely inconsistent and depends on which reviews or individual studies are viewed. A 1999 study found that attendance of AA was worse than no treatment. However, another analysis found that rates of abstinence are about twice as high among those who attend AA. It's truly a mixed bag in terms of what research and individual accounts you look at.

Ultimately, how helpful you find the program likely depends on the way you practice it and how seriously you take it—and to be frank, how much you feel that abstinence is right for you. For those in AA, engagement in the 12 steps is important and associated with abstinence outcomes. For example, participants with both drug and alcohol dependency who had a sponsor had read 12-step literature, were involved with service work, called other members for help, and were almost three times more likely than those less involved to maintain abstinence at two years.

But abstinence is only one option for treatment. Some people find abstinence to be extreme. For others, particularly those who find they have an all-or-nothing approach to their use—and an increase in risk-taking behaviors when they take their preferred substance—it may be a good option for those very reasons. If this describes you and you feel like your use is more compulsive than functional—that is, you become a different person when you're using, and not one you necessarily like—you might consider the 12-step focus on abstinence beneficial, and something you want to pursue.

Harm Reduction

If abstinence seems like a high or unnecessary bar considering your substance use and how it functions in your life, know that other treatments have been developed which do not have standards that can seem that rigid. This is where harm reduction can be useful.

Harm reduction is a framework for addressing substance use and other potentially risky behaviors that aims to reduce the consequences of these behaviors without requiring users to abstain entirely. It is an alternative to traditional abstinence-only treatments and extends the reach of treatment to substance users who are unwilling or unable to stop using. Harm reduction was developed both in reaction to abstinence programs and of activism in the United

States related to criminalization of drug use behaviors in the 1980s, which remain differentially enforced among disenfranchised and discriminated groups.

In 2010, Drs. Andrew Tatarsky and G. Alan Marlatt described the clinical principles of harm reduction, which are as follows. (Note that the principles were initially written for clinicians working with clients; I have adapted these ideas into principles you can use on your own.)

1. Substance use problems are best understood and addressed in the context of the whole person in their social environment. (This is in contrast to certain models of addiction treatment that focus exclusively on substance use or addiction as a problem, rather than considering how the substance use functions in the user's life.)

2. You have strengths that can be supported.

3. It's vital for the culture at large and for psychotherapy to challenge the stigmatization of substance use.

4. Substances are used for adaptive reasons—that is, they're used to make life easier to live; they don't reflect weakness in the user's life or wrongdoing on the user's part.

5. Drug use falls on a continuum of harmful consequences; it's not all-or-nothing.

6. It's key to not hold abstinence (or any other preconceived notions) as a precondition.

7. Engagement in treatment/change—not abstinence—is the primary goal.

8. Look for and mobilize your strengths in service of change.

Although the above principles are centered on how you can use harm reduction in your work with a therapist, there are also ways to practice harm reduction on your own. Let's think about some ways you can use harm reduction principles regarding your use on your own.

Practicing Harm Reduction

First, consider if or how you'd like to reduce your use. Think about what you might do to gain more control over when and how you use substance(s). If you use substances every-day, for instance, consider how you might cut back. For example, one client who drank alcohol every day decided to just drink on Fridays, Saturdays, and Sundays. Another person who used cocaine all weekend decided to just use on Saturday. What ways could you change your use to make it more manageable?

_____

_____

_____

_____

Next, consider the circumstances in which you use substances. Consider your environment, including using only in a safe place and with people that you trust and who use safely. If you find that you take risks while using with certain people, can you limit your exposure to them? How might you change your environment to make taking substances safer?

_____

_____

_____

_____

Here are some steps for harm reduction specific to alcohol use:

- Never drink on an empty stomach.

- Don't drink more than two drinks in three hours.

- Don't drink alcohol in place of calories you'd otherwise get from food; only drink alcohol with food.

- Drink a glass of water for every drink of alcohol.

- Drink one drink at a time (try not to have a shot with a beer, for example).

- When in groups, try to not feel pressure to keep up. It's okay to drink less than others.

- Although this is socially common, avoid the temptation to drink shots at the end of the night. If you do, take one and sip it slowly.

- Consider asking your doctor about medications that can reduce alcohol cravings or that make alcohol less pleasant.

- Plan alcohol-free days; notice if you feel better on these days.

- On days you do drink, consider not drinking until later in the day, eventually pushing back the starting time.

And here are recommendations for harm reduction specific to drug use:

- Avoid mixing substances; for example, don't use alcohol with other drugs.

- Don't share needles, and use clean ones. Most cities in the US have needle exchanges, where you can get supplies for free, without judgment.

- Avoid using alone.

- Ask your doctor about a prescription for Narcan (naxolone), which can reverse opioid overdose.

- Practice with taking less, even if it's just a little.

- Ask your doctor about medications that can reduce cravings.

- If you are planning a night of drug use, consider who you will be with, and set limits on adding new members to your group to increase chances of your being safe.

Finally, here are recommendations for harm reduction for all kinds of substance use:

- Recall strategies for managing anxiety and depression and grounding which have been described in this book. Sometimes, it can be helpful to use one of these strategies in lieu of or in addition to your substances.

- Get enough sleep and practice good sleep hygiene.

- Exercise; move your body as much as you can.

- Find supportive people who support your desire to take fewer substances.

- Use meditation if it works for you.

- Use distraction and pleasurable activities to avoid cravings.

- Try to identify your triggers related to PTSD or CPTSD and find other ways to cope with those.

- When in groups, there are usually predictable times when people take substances in extreme excess. Try to buddy up with someone who wants to have a relatively mellow time and will use less with you.

Ultimately, you may find that working a 12-step program or practicing harm reduction principles can help you get to where you want to be with your substance use. Ideally this is a place where your use functions to make your symptoms easier to deal with, without becoming overwhelming or problematic for you. You may also find that these solo treatment options don't feel like enough for you; you're struggling to stick to the changes you want to make, or your substance use still feels maladaptive or problematic in some way. If so, there are steps you can take to get help.

What to Do If You Can't Do It on Your Own

If you're seeking help, you can consider both inpatient or outpatient facilities that help people who have excessive and problematic drug or alcohol use. Another option is to find a therapist who specializes in substance abuse, ideally one who is trauma informed and willing to work with you regarding flexible techniques, and with whom you can decide how you want to get your use under better control. Although getting the right therapist can be a life-changing experience, it can also be a struggle to find a clinician who is the right fit. I'll give you some tools do so in the next chapter.

Conclusion

Substance use can often be related to PTSD and CPTSD. It's helpful to have an understanding about your relationship with substances so you can determine if and how you might want to change that relationship in any way. Substances may be serving as self-medication, and to gather further data points, it's good to understand what you've found useful about using drugs or alcohol. At the same time, it's helpful to know that there are limits to what substances can provide. Ultimately, the primary use for substances is in coping with overwhelming feelings in the moment or the short term; they are not healing in terms of long-term recovery. In the end, though, your journey is yours to decide. It's your call how you'd like to understand and change your relationship with substances.

CHAPTER 9

Finding a Therapist
Using Research to Find the Best Fit

Even with resources like this workbook and a very supportive social network, many find it useful at some point to see a professional who can help. As I said in the introduction, this book necessarily covers only the first part of treatment for CPTSD, which is understanding the neurobiology of trauma (fight/flight/freeze) and creating a basic sense of safety for yourself in your life; learning healthier coping skills for intrusive experiences of fear, anger, and anxiety; building the basics of metacognition; and building social support to help you deal with your CPTSD. The second part of treatment—dealing with the memories of your traumatic experience through exposure therapy, EMDR, psychodynamic therapy, and other techniques—is something a professional can help you with, because it is beyond the scope of this workbook. And you may not need or want to take this step, depending on your particular experience of CPTSD.

This chapter will help you move on to that next stage of your life and recovery. It will describe what researchers think makes therapy work and how you might find someone who can help you, if you decide you are ready for that. As this is ultimately more about the fit between the client and therapist than technique, I'll provide tools to help you assess therapists to find the best person for you to work with.

Depending on where you live, there may be a lot of therapists or only a few. Here's something that's true, but tough to digest: even if you live in an area where there are thousands of therapists, it can be challenging to find people qualified to treat CPTSD, for several reasons. Literature, treatment recommendations, and research on CPTSD are still emerging. There can be some confusion among professionals regarding whether complex trauma equates to a personality disorder; this is important as it can impact the way a therapist treats you or even how they respond to your concerns. My position on this is that CPTSD and personality disorders do not have to be parallel. I'm also personally wary of diagnosing anyone with a personality disorder—there are just so many problems with this diagnostic category because of how we measure it using available statistics. There's no one-size-fits-all assessment. It's true that understanding someone's character and the ways their background has informed their coping styles and personality traits are important, and it is vital that a therapist can understand many aspects of you, including the ways you may have adapted to protect yourself. But this does not have to be linked with a personality disorder diagnosis, which I consider to be unhelpful and unnecessary in most cases.

Further, it's important to note that the field of psychology has become increasingly focused on technique. While that is not necessarily a bad thing—we should think about what works for whom—some therapists and researchers have become a bit inflexible about specific techniques that should be used for all people. This is where things can get a bit problematic. First, we are all complicated human beings, no matter what our history is and no matter our symptoms; we are all distinct and need different things when we seek therapy. When a therapist is too focused on one or two techniques, or even just methods in general, there can be problems. As the old saying goes, "When the only tool you have is a hammer, everything looks like a nail." In other words: some clinicians can be so focused on techniques they forget to think about the whole person in front of them. Additionally, if a therapist is wedded to using one or two clinical techniques, they may have trouble seeing when something is not working. My belief is that clients need clinicians who can pivot and try another approach when something does not work.

That said, a focus on technique may not always be negative. If you have done your research, you may say, for example, "I want someone who just does EMDR. That could work for me, and I want to try it with a specialist." If that is the case, that's great. But a lot of times, as clients, we may not know what we want. We may not even know that there are so many different methods of therapy to choose from! So, it's important to consider finding a therapist who knows multiple ways of helping people. It's also crucial to find a therapist with whom you'll have a good working relationship. As you will see, methods the therapist uses do matter, but success in treatment depends largely on how safe you feel with the person you entrust your care to. And this leads us to this question: What indicates a successful therapy relationship?

What Predicts Success in Therapy?

Decades of research supports that the therapy relationship is the most important factor in therapy outcome, more than the technique used. Specifically, therapeutic relationship factors constitute about 30 percent of psychotherapy outcomes, while techniques (the method of therapy conducted) account for 15 percent of outcomes. This means the relationship between client and therapist is thought to contribute *twice as much* to therapeutic change than the techniques we employ. Although there is a lot that is hard to quantify in terms of what makes a therapy relationship work, researchers think that empathy may be an important part of the equation. When we feel our therapists are empathic and sensitive regarding our suffering, it results in better outcomes. And if you think about this from an attachment perspective, this makes a great deal of sense. The more securely attached we feel to our therapists, the more it is likely that we can reveal the most personal and vulnerable aspects of our experience— slowly and over time. Feeling safe is key. It does take time, even with people we like.

And to state the obvious, something that is really important is that *you like your therapist.* I know it might seem weird to say that, but I can't tell you how many people I know who stuck with a clinician they did not really care for because of pressures they felt. Such pressures can be external, like when a therapist nudges someone to stay. They can also be internal. For instance, sometimes people with trauma histories don't feel entitled to be with someone who makes them feel cared for. Therapy is hard and involves a lot of painful emotions, but it does not mean that you shouldn't pick someone you simply just click with.

Research has broken this down a bit more in terms of looking at what factors contribute to a successful therapy relationship. Referred to as "common factors" in the research, these factors may explain a great deal of why and how therapy works. This means things that encompass the therapeutic alliance: empathy, goal consensus and collaboration, positive regard and affirmation, mastery, genuineness, and mentalization, meaning what we as therapists do that can be ultimately more helpful, like being able to imagine what might be going on with you. Also, therapists who are skilled at talking with people from a variety of backgrounds have better success with their clients. The same line of research suggests that it's important that clients find their therapists to be authentic and easy to relate to, with a good dose of humility. Personally, I also find humor to be an important part of the dynamic in successful therapy relationships. Yes, you are in therapy to work, but part of that work is to feel pleasure at times in the connection with the person you are seeing. Know that therapy doesn't need to always be serious; in fact, it probably shouldn't be. It's not only okay, but often neces-sary to laugh and experience joy at times.

Regarding this point, it's important that none of us in my field take ourselves too seriously or act as if we are perfect. Some clinicians have approached our work with more than a mild dose of hubris, which can make clients feel judged or like their faults amount to more than their strengths. I have felt this way myself when I have been a patient in therapy and I don't want this for you. So, it's important that you feel a healthy sense of entitlement when you think about choosing a therapist. Think of it this way: *Good therapists should be able to offer a number of ways to help you, and to the extent that it is possible, you have a right to feel safe and comforted in their presence.*

All of this is to say the fit between therapist and client is about multiple factors—some of which relate to techniques therapists use, and some of which relate to the natural connection you might form with a professional you work with. As a prospective client/consumer, you also have the right to know about the different kinds of treatments that are offered and what we understand about how therapy works. Therapists have many different styles of working and many different personalities, so it's important to think about what style might work best for you.

Setting Intentions: Finding the Best Therapist for You with C-NIP

This next exercise is designed to get you thinking about the kinds of the kinds of things you may or may not want in a therapist. The instrument we'll use, the Cooper-Norcross Inventory of Preferences (C-NIP), was designed by Drs. Mick Cooper and John Norcross and is used here with their permission. It helps you gauge the degree to which you do or don't prefer aspects of therapist attitude. These aspects are *directiveness,* or whether you'd like your therapist to lead you in treatment or to direct treatment yourself; *emotional intensity,* or the degree to which you'd like to have a personal relationship with your therapist or maintain a degree of reserve; *past or present orientation,* or whether you'd prefer if treatment focused more on the past or on the present or future; and *warm support* versus *focused challenge,* which has to do with how much support you'd prefer from a professional you work with and the nature of that support—whether you want a professional you work with to support you unconditionally or to challenge you in certain ways. The C-NIP is also downloadable at https://www.c-nip.net/.

Cooper – Norcross Inventory of Preferences (C-NIP) v1.1

On each of the items below, please indicate your preferences for how a psychotherapist or counsellor should work with you by circling a number. A 3 indicates a *strong* preference in that direction, 2 indicates a *moderate* preference in that direction, 1 indicates a *slight* preference in that direction, 0 indicates no preference in either direction/an equally strong preference in both directions.

'I would like the therapist to…'

1. Focus on specific goals

    No or equal preference

    Not focus on specific goals

3	2	1	0	-1	-2	-3

2. Give structure to the therapy

    No or equal preference

    Allow the therapy to be unstructured

3	2	1	0	-1	-2	-3

3. Teach me skills to deal with my problems

    No or equal preference

    Not teach me skills to deal with my problems

3	2	1	0	-1	-2	-3

4. Give me 'homework' to do

    No or equal preference

    Not give me 'homework' to do

3	2	1	0	-1	-2	-3

5. Take a lead in therapy

    No or equal preference

    Allow me to take a lead in therapy

3	2	1	0	-1	-2	-3

Scale 1. If score is 8 to 15 then strong preference for therapist directiveness. If score is -2 to 7 then no strong preference. If score is -3 to -15 then strong preference for client directiveness.

6. Encourage me to go into difficult emotions

    No or equal preference

    Not encourage me to go into difficult emotions

3	2	1	0	-1	-2	-3

7. Talk with me about the therapy relationship

No or equal preference

Not talk with me about the therapy relationship

    3   2   1   0   -1   -2   -3

8. Focus on the relationship between us

No or equal preference

Not focus on the relationship between us

    3   2   1   0   -1   -2   -3

9. Encourage me to express strong feelings

No or equal preference

Not encourage me to express strong feelings

    3   2   1   0   -1   -2   -3

10. Focus mainly on my feelings

No or equal preference

Focus mainly on my thoughts

    3   2   1   0   -1   -2   -3

Scale 2. If score is 7 to 15 then strong preference for emotional intensity. If score is 0 to 6 then no strong preference. If score is -15 to -1 then strong preference for emotional reserve

11. Focus on my life in the past

No or equal preference

Focus on my life in the present

    3   2   1   0   -1   -2   -3

12. Help me reflect on my childhood

No or equal preference

Help me reflect on my adulthood

    3   2   1   0   -1   -2   -3

Scale 3. If score is 3 to 9 then strong preference for past orientation. If score is -2 to 2 then no strong preference. If score is -3 to -9 then strong preference for present orientation.

13. Focus on my past

No or equal preference

Focus on my future

    3   2   1   0   -1   -2   -3

14. Be gentle   No or equal preference   Be challenging

| 3 | 2 | 1 | 0 | -1 | -2 | -3 |

15. Be supportive   No or equal preference   Be confrontational

| 3 | 2 | 1 | 0 | -1 | -2 | -3 |

16. Not interrupt me   No or equal preference   Interrupt me and keep me focused

| 3 | 2 | 1 | 0 | -1 | -2 | -3 |

17. Not be challenging of my own beliefs and views   No or equal preference   Be challenging of my own beliefs and views

| 3 | 2 | 1 | 0 | -1 | -2 | -3 |

18. Support my behavior unconditionally   No or equal preference   Challenge my behaviour if they think it's wrong

| 3 | 2 | 1 | 0 | -1 | -2 | -3 |

Scale 4. If score is 4 to 15 then strong preference for warm support, If score is -3 to 3 then no strong preference. If score is -4 to -15 then strong preference for focused challenge.

Additional client preferences for exploration and consideration (as appropriate to service provision)

Do you have a strong preference for:

- A therapist of a particular **gender, race/ethnicity, sexual orientation, religion,** or **other personal characteristic**?

- A therapist/counsellor who speaks a **specific language** that is most comfortable for you?

- **Modality** of therapy: such as individual, couple, family, or group therapy?

- **Orientation** of therapy: such as psychodynamic, cognitive, person-centered, or other?

- **Number** of therapy sessions: such as four, dependent on review, open-ended, or other?

- **Length** of therapy sessions: such as 50 mins, 60 mins, 90 mins, or other?

- **Frequency** of therapy: such as twice weekly, weekly, monthly, ad hoc, or other?

- **Medication**, psychotherapy, or both in combination?

- Use of **self-help** books, self-help groups, or computer programs in addition to therapy?

- **Any other** strong preferences that come to mind? (and do raise them at any point in therapy)

- What would you most **dislike** or **despise** happening in your therapy or counselling?

What did you find out about your preferences? Do you want someone who talks a lot or mostly listens? Someone who gives homework or who can be less structured? One of the things I find most helpful about this instrument is that it provides so many things to consider about a therapeutic relationship. I love how it puts the power in *your* hands, allowing you to think about what you want and then hopefully feel empowered when you interview potential therapists to work with.

The one thing I would add to the C-NIP, which you may want to think about, is the issue of revisiting trauma memories. Consider whether this might be something you are interested in, and let a prospective therapist know if you are or are not willing to deal with trauma memories, as this can be really helpful for you to state at the outset of a new therapeutic relationship. If a therapist insists that you deal with trauma memories, especially early on in treatment, and you are not ready to do that, consider finding a different therapist.

Types of Therapies to Consider

There are a number of techniques that can be used by therapists and it's important to consider the preferences you might have. In service of that, let's go over some common forms of therapy and define them.

Acceptance and Commitment Therapy (ACT)

Acceptance and commitment therapy (ACT) encourages people to live and behave in ways that match personal values, while promoting psychological flexibility. The goal is to help individuals recognize ways in which their attempts to ignore and control their emotional experiences—trying to suppress thoughts they don't want, avoiding situations that might provoke them, and so on—can make things difficult and limit their ability to live a fulfilling life. ACT does not attempt to directly change or stop unwanted thoughts or feelings (in contrast to cognitive behavior therapy, which we'll discuss in the next section). ACT is more about learning how to experience unwanted thoughts and feelings in such a way that they no longer keep you from doing the things that give your life value.

Cognitive Behavioral Therapy (CBT)

Cognitive behavioral therapy is fixed specifically on the relationship between thoughts, feelings, and behaviors. It focuses on specific symptoms and asks clients to record and keep track of various thoughts and related mood states. Given how wide and nuanced various CBT approaches have become, the approach used can vary, with some clinicians emphasizing cognitive versus behavioral aspects. However, note that therapies which emphasize cognitive treatment for trauma are focused on changing beliefs and ideas related to the traumatic events themselves.

The American Psychological Association discusses certain underlying theories under the umbrella of CBT for PTSD (not necessarily CPTSD). For example, they highlight *emotional processing theory,* which focuses on changing associations to the traumatic event. *Social cognitive theory* focuses on adjusting "maladaptive" beliefs that are associated with traumatic events. *Cognitive therapy for PTSD* is similar to CBT, though the focus is more on changing perceptions that are considered "pessimistic," and the aim is to alter ideas of the traumatic event.

CBT techniques are often assumed to include exposure therapies, as discussed in chapter 6. *Prolonged exposure therapy* or PE addresses the symptom of avoidance. Advocates of this approach believe that avoiding reminders of the trauma increases the traumatic event's strength for clients, because fear is reinforced. Exposures are initiated early in treatment with the idea that clients can learn that cues and thoughts related to the traumatic event are not inherently dangerous. *Cognitive processing therapy* on the other hand, reduces the amount of exposure time clients need to endure while focusing on altering "unhelpful" beliefs related to the trauma.

Dialectical Behavior Therapy (DBT)

While some describe DBT as a form of cognitive behavioral therapy, it's a very distinct way of helping people who have more intense difficulties with emotional regulation, including harmful behaviors (such as cutting) or frequent suicidal ideation. DBT involves the teaching of a number of skills that promote self-regulation and mindfulness.

Eye Movement Desensitization Reprocessing

EMDR is thought by some to be a kind of exposure therapy, and its efficacy has been found to be comparable to exposure treatments for those with PTSD, not necessarily CPTSD, though there is ongoing research to determine how helpful EMDR is for people with CPTSD. EMDR is said to work by enhancing the processing of the trauma because of new connections that are made when focusing on a vivid image while pairing this with eye movements, tones, tapping, or other kinds of tactile stimulation.

Person-Centered Therapy and Humanistic Therapy

Person-centered therapy and *humanistic therapy* are closely related, with the former being developed by Carl Rogers eighty years ago; the latter emphasizes looking at people in their entirety, not just symptoms of illness or disease. Both theories stress concepts such as free will and self-efficacy, while helping people build on and maximize their potential. These therapies focus on client strengths while using empathy and positive regard to provide a sense of safety where a client can realize their potential for growth.

Psychodynamic Therapy

Psychodynamic therapy is related to psychoanalysis, which is the oldest form of therapy, pioneered by Sigmund Freud. Psychodynamic therapy is now very diverse, but in general tends to the understanding of emotions and thoughts that may not be readily apparent, as well as recurring patterns in behavior, especially in regard to relationships. Many psychodynamic therapists, though not all, believe that talking about early family dynamics is an important part of healing.

I realize that these choices may seem dizzying, especially if you have not been in therapy before. It's important to do your own research but consider how the style of therapy may or may not fit your personality and your personal goals. For example, if you are interested in thinking about your values and have a sense you are constantly fighting off your emotions, ACT could be an approach to try. If you are not very interested in spending a great deal of time with your emotions and would like concrete strategies, behavioral approaches could be a good fit. If you are interested in a deeper understanding of yourself and are especially interested in understanding dynamics of your family and childhood, then psychodynamic therapy could be a helpful treatment. Make sure to remember that the most important part of therapy is the relationship between you and your provider. I hope that can make you feel less pressure when choosing to try someone out if you are seeking therapy, because depending on your preference and needs, you may simply want to find someone you get along with in addition to considering their therapeutic methodology. Finally, as both a clinician and a patient, I feel that it's helpful to find a therapist who has more than one or two tools in their toolbox.

Whatever you may be looking for, let's take a moment to think about that first session with a new therapist and how you might determine if they are a good fit.

How to Handle That First Session

How should you assess the first visit with a new therapist? This is a tough question; the most basic way to answer it is just to *trust your instincts*. That said, there are some things we can put into use to get you thinking about that first visit and what you might look for. Also, keep in mind it can take several sessions to know if a therapist is a good fit. However, many people do make an assessment about whether to continue based on just one session. Therapy is expensive and takes up time, so it's reasonable to make the most of the initial session.

If you filled out the C-NIP questionnaire, you likely already have some great things to consider about what you can look for in a therapist. It's good to keep those things in mind. When you meet with someone for the first time, try to consider the things that seem most important to you to start with and goals you have; however, I'd suggest just starting with talking about yourself and assess how the therapist listens. Is it easy(ish) to talk with them? Is there a somewhat natural back and forth? Do you feel heard and understood?

If you have an extensive trauma history, I'd suggest that you mention this in the initial session but avoid going into too much detail until you know the clinician better. I have heard stories of people going in for a first session and saying things before they were ready, which they later regretted. Remember, trauma often involves long and somewhat disjointed narratives that should be expressed in very safe company. You have a right to comfort and safety within your own experience.

We'll think of some ways you can assess your experience with a therapist in what I will call a first session checklist, though you may want to wait until after the first few sessions to complete it, depending on your experience.

First Sessions Checklist

First sessions are often awkward—but there are some criteria you can use to evaluate them. Consider the following about your experience after meeting someone for the first time or the first few times, and circle Yes or No as appropriate. (A download of this assessment, if you need it, is available at http://www.newharbinger.com/49708.)

The therapist offered some initial ideas about how to start:	Yes	No
Seemed empathic about how hard it might be for me to start talking:	Yes	No
Something about their presence made me feel safe right away:	Yes	No
The therapist talked when I wanted them to:	Yes	No
I felt good in the office and liked the space/video setting:	Yes	No
The therapist seemed to be listening:	Yes	No
They redirected me in a way that was helpful:	Yes	No
They seemed to get me:	Yes	No
They explained what their general treatment methods are:	Yes	No
They seemed confident without being arrogant:	Yes	No
They could admit when they did not know something:	Yes	No
I felt I had some access to their thoughts about me:	Yes	No
They made comments which indicated they were empathic:	Yes	No
The therapist asked what kind of therapy I might prefer:	Yes	No
They asked what kinds of therapy I'd tried before (e.g., already tried CBT):	Yes	No
They had a sense of possible goals and issues at the end of the first session:	Yes	No

I realize this is a very ambitious checklist. You should keep in mind it can take a while to get to know anyone, especially a therapist. One session may not nearly be enough to know if it's the right fit. But the more "yes" answers you have, the greater the number of indicators that you're off to a good start.

Although I am suggesting a more experiential first session, you might find that a more direct approach works better for you. For example, you can opt to ask your therapist what kind of clients they like working with and what their professional background is—though many of us now do this online, through our websites. One idea regarding the latter point: many clients have told me over the years that the more specific a therapist's website is, the more they can get a sense of them. Therefore, consider it a good sign if therapists have details about whom they work with.

Also, keep in mind that if you want to have a number of sessions, be sure to be clear about fees, insurance, and cancellation policies. I do think it's important to ask what kinds of therapy the clinician provides if you have not done it already. Again, I think it's useful for trauma survivors to find therapists who have a number of techniques they can offer you, to not limit your treatment.

Even when things may start off right with a therapist, you may sense after a few sessions in that it's just not working. It's important to remember that you can leave anytime. But remember that it can take a while to find a rhythm with a therapist, even when things are going well. Let's think about the ways you can have the best experience, which may require you to be able to assert yourself.

Getting What You Need: Practicing Assertiveness with Your Treatment Provider

It's important to make the most of your time in treatment. This may sound confusing, since therapy is most successful when we have patience and allow time for trust to develop. People can err on either side, by staying too long in a therapy that is not the right fit, or leaving without giving therapy a chance to work. It's not easy to jump from one therapist to another, and it's emotionally difficult; clients often say, "It takes so long to tell my story! I hate to start over!" This makes total sense. Avoiding this situation starts with you being able to ask for what you need.

As you may already know, it can be hard to be honest with your therapist. Our clinicians are in a position of authority and we often need them and we want to be liked by them. Yet research has found that up to 72 percent of psychotherapy clients had lied about their therapy experience. Common mistruths included pretending to agree with the therapist's suggestions, pretending to find treatment helpful, masking their opinion of the therapist, and not being honest about why they missed or were late to sessions. I can understand why it's so hard to be honest with your therapist, but it's crucial to getting the best care possible. First, if your therapist does not know what you need, it can be more difficult for them to help. But there is another important reason to be honest. Many who have traumatic backgrounds have never had the space to say what is on their minds or complain. It's likely that many abusive people in your life have dismissed you because you voiced that you were upset or hurt. But asserting concerns is vital in *all* relationships. No one ever gets it right all the time and even the people we love the most disappoint us. We should be able to speak to this in a meaningful way that is heard and understood. Even if the other person may not agree with our complaints, it's important to feel that they are at least considered.

Here are some important tips for being assertive with your therapist:

1. Speak openly and focus on how you feel, without making judgments about motives. This opens the space for better mutual understanding even as it makes clear that something has happened that may need to change going forward.

2. If you don't feel heard or understood, provide a specific example in which your therapist missed the mark.

3. Think about what you need in terms of how and how much the therapist talks to you and gives you feedback. Tell them if you need more feedback; tell them if you need them to give you more time to talk.

4. If you don't like homework and know you won't do it, state this outright. A qualified therapist should be able to offer therapy without homework if that is not right for you.

5. On the other hand, sometimes, clients want homework. If you find you want more than your therapist is providing, discuss how or if they can accommodate this.

6. Ask your therapist ahead of time how you might discuss the feedback you'd like to give, and the best way to provide feedback.

7. A related idea is to establish regular check-ins for you regarding how you feel therapy is going for you.

8. If memories come up in your therapy and/or your therapist is pressing you to discuss them, take some time to think about it, and slow it down if it's too much. This is because once you discover hidden memories it's easy to quickly go down a rabbit hole of recalling unpleasant events, which can lead to overwhelm. Timing is an important and ongoing aspect of your treatment.

9. Analyze the therapist—to some extent. If you bring up a concern or a complaint and the therapist has trouble hearing it, or can't take in your ideas about what might be more useful for you, then it may be better to part ways.

Being assertive in therapy is important because what we do with our therapists is a way to practice how to take care of ourselves in life. As a trauma survivor, you know how hard it is to stand up for yourself in a genuine, thoughtful, and non-aggressive way. Therapy is a testing ground in which we get to practice the skills we'll eventually bring into our lives. It may be hard to know how and when to leave a therapy relationship, but in general, trust your instincts. You likely know what you need.

Conclusion

A therapeutic relationship is intensely personal and it's difficult to explain it from the outside of it. Only you will know if you have found the right fit. Good therapy should be both easy *and* hard. It should be easy in that you shouldn't have to worry about taking care of your provider, or that saying what is on your mind will overly impact your therapist. And it should be easy to feel safe even when you know you might be misconstruing things; that is, you should feel you have someone on your side who can help you reconstruct your perspective when that's necessary. Therapy is hard, though, in that it's a space to discuss the most difficult aspects of your life. So, balance is key. Therapy is work; it can also be fun. If you decide to pursue it, remember to trust your instincts. Know that it's okay to laugh with the person who you are in treatment with, and above all, it's vital that you always consider how safe you feel.

Continuing on the Road to Healing

As you come to the end of this book, it is important to acknowledge just how hard you have worked and the struggles you've had to overcome to think about your life, your trauma, and your symptoms. Whether this is the first time you have come to face your relationship with complex trauma or if you have been dealing with its impact on your life and self-concept for a long time, just considering your struggles and the ways you have coped is a great gift you have given yourself.

I'll say it once more: Trauma is identity theft—and it shifts the foundation of so many things that others may take for granted, such as safety, security, a sense of wholeness and confidence, and the ability to know who you are and how you really feel. However, in my thirty years of practice, I have come to believe that trauma survivors are incredibly resilient and remarkable. People who undergo adversity think outside of the box, and often perceive things that others miss. Many people who have endured trauma not only go on to live in the world, they contribute to society in outstanding ways. They are often truth-tellers and wisdom-seekers, and they can become great mentors and advisors. One big reason to take your healing seriously is so you can give back. I hope your narrative eventually becomes the story of how you help and heal yourself and others.

As a trauma survivor, you are likely empathic and sensitive to the needs of others. As I've described, at times this can manifest as hypervigilance—paying intense attention to the needs of others as a necessary cognitive and emotional skill—but you can learn that focusing on yourself won't leave you in danger. In fact, it will make you better prepared, both internally and externally, for the challenges life holds. It's all about learning to understand your own mind and instincts, and also to manage what you experience and feel.

We've discussed that you already possess the tools for growth. You can harness skills like mentalization, which can help you understand how to use your mind to facilitate emotional thinking; empathy for yourself and others; insight; and the ability to control and manage your emotions. And yes, at times your body and mind may make this difficult; it can be easy to be reminded of trauma. The fight/flight/freeze response will likely challenge you when you are under stress. But you've learned vital tools to manage this, and you'll continue to learn as you heal. And when it comes to healing: therapy is recommended if you want to look at specific aspects of your trauma background, particularly if are interested in seeing if exposure or other ways of exploring your trauma may be right for you.

Your Journey Continues

Healing from complex trauma takes place over a lifetime. As you progress through different stages of life—commitments in long-term relationships, having children, career challenges and success, the loss of parents or other loved ones, middle age, old age—you will face different reminders of trauma. You'll need to use your tools to adapt to novel obstacles. At times it may seem as if you have found a comfortable plateau in your struggles, but then suddenly it's like there's another hill to climb. But no matter how hard things get, you can come back to this book—or just look inward and remember that you can harness the most resilient aspects of yourself and your identity.

Part of your recovery is remembering that as a trauma survivor, you need to be cautious about who you let into your life and who gains your trust. Sometimes our challenges have to do with wanting to believe that someone we care about has our best interest in mind when this may not be the case. Healing involves listening to our inner voice, trusting our instincts, and knowing when we need to let go of certain relationships to make room for people who will nourish us and grow with us.

It can be hard to feel entitled to a good life given all that you have been through. I get that. There's a saying I have shared with many clients, and I'll share it with you now: *There may have been people who have not cared or who have even not wanted you to find happiness. You're an adult now, though. And the universe does not take away good things from people who find joy or pleasure. There is enough good to go around, and you deserve your place in a good life.*

Resources

As you continue on the road to healing from complex trauma, here are some resources that might be valuable. It's far from an exhaustive list; generally, I've tried to cover groups that may experience adult trauma, including veterans, first responders, and survivors of domestic violence and sexual assault. There are also resources for people who have experienced childhood adversity and neglect as well as the major hotlines for people dealing with a suicidal crisis. Additionally, support for people of color and LGBTQ+ communities is included in this list, as is support for immigrants and refugees. Finally, there are some resources on finding a therapist. I incorporated resources in the United States, Canada, Australia, and the United Kingdom.

Suicide Hotlines and Prevention Resources

United States of America

National Emergency: 911

National Suicide Prevention Lifeline (http://suicidepreventionlifeline.org): 1-800-273-8255

 Nacional de Prevención del Suicidio: 1-888-628-9454 (ayuda en español)

Essential Community Services: 211

 Hotline can also be reached by texting to 838255

Samaritans USA (http://www.samaritansusa.org/programs.php): offers hotlines and support groups

Crisis Text Line (https://www.crisistextline.org/): Text HOME to 741 741 for free, 24/7 crisis counseling

United Kingdom

National Emergency: 112 or 999

111, Option 2: National Health Services' First Response Service for mental health crises and support

*not available in all areas of the UK yet

Samaritans (UK Hotline) (http://www.samaritans.org/): +44 (0) 8457 90 90 90 (UK – local rate)

Samaritans Helpline: 116 123

Campaign Against Living Miserably (https://www.thecalmzone.net)

CALM (Nationwide): 0800 58 58 58 (available every day from 5 p.m. to midnight)

CALM (London): 0808 802 58 58 (available every day from 5 p.m. to midnight)

CALM Webchat: https://www.thecalmzone.net/help/get-help/ (available every day from 5 p.m. to midnight)

ROI Hotline: 1850 60 90 90

Support Line: https://www.supportline.org.uk/problems/suicide/

Shout (https://giveusashout.org/): Text SHOUT to 85258

Ireland

National Emergency: 112 and 999

Samaritans: Freephone 116 123 anywhere in Ireland or Northern Ireland

50808

(https://text50808.ie) is a free, confidential 24/7 national crisis-intervention text-message service. It can be reached by texting **HELLO** to **50808**.

Canada

National Emergency: 911

Canada Suicide Prevention Service (http://www.crisisservicescanada.ca):
1-833-456-4566 or 45645; text available 4 p.m. to midnight ET only

Kids Help Phone (https://kidshelpphone.ca)

Free 24/7 national support service that provides confidential professional counselling, information, referrals and volunteer-led, text-based support to young
people in both English and French

Crisis Text Line (https://www.crisistextline.ca): Text HOME (English) or PARLER
(French) to 686868

Canadian Association for Suicide Prevention: https://suicideprevention.ca
/Need-Help

Australia

National Emergency: 000

Lifeline: 13 11 14; https://www.lifeline.org.au

24-hour nationwide services providing access to crisis support, suicide prevention and mental health support services

Online chat services open every day from 7 p.m. to midnight Sydney time

Kids Helpline: 1800 55 1800 ; https://kidshelpline.com.au

24-hour nationwide service providing access to crisis support, suicide prevention
and counselling services for Australians ages 5-25; also offers online chat
services

Beyond Blue: 1300 22 4636 to reach their 24/7 hotline; they also offer an online
chat from 3 p.m. to midnight every day; https://www.beyondblue.org.au

Suicide Call Back Service (https://www.suicidecallbackservice.org.au): 1300 659 467

Also offers online chat and video chat services

Veterans Resources

United States of America

U.S. Department of Veterans Affairs: https://www.va.gov

Mental Health Resources: https://www.mentalhealth.va.gov/index.asp

National Center for PTSD: https://www.ptsd.va.gov

National Call Center for Homeless Veterans: 1-877-4AID VET (877-424-3838); https://www.va.gov/homeless/nationalcallcenter.asp

Vet Centers (Readjustment Counseling): https://www.vetcenter.va.gov

Mental Health Resources: https://www.mentalhealth.gov/get-help/veterans

Veteran Crisis Line: Call 1-800-273-8255 and press 1, available 24/7; https://www.veteranscrisisline.net

By July 2022, the hotline will be available to reach by dialing **988**

Military OneSource: 1-800-342-9647, available 24/7; https://www.military onesource.mil

National Alliance on Mental Illness: https://www.nami.org/Your-Journey /Veterans-Active-Duty

Marine Corps DSTRESS Line: Anonymous Marine-to-Marine phone and chat support service; 1-877-476-7734, available 24/7

United Kingdom

Veterans' Gateway: https://support.veteransgateway.org.uk/ https://www.veteransgateway.org.uk/mental-wellbeing-advice-for-veterans

Canada

Veterans Affairs Canada: https://www.veterans.gc.ca/eng/health-support

Australia

Department of Veterans' Affairs Mental Health Support Services:
https://www.dva.gov.au/health-and-treatment/injury-or-health-treatments
/mental-health-care/mental-health-support-services

Resources for Survivors of Sexual Assault and Domestic Violence

United States of America

National Center of Domestic Violence, Trauma & Mental Health:
http://www.nationalcenterdvtraumamh.org/resources/national-domestic-
violence-organizations

RAINN (Rape, Abuse, & Incest National Network): https://www.rainn.org

   Online Hotline: https://hotline.rainn.org/online

   National Sexual Assault Hotline: 1-800-656-HOPE (4673)

National Domestic Violence Hotline: 1-800-799-SAFE (7233), live chat and more
information at https://www.thehotline.org

   Teletype (TTY) Hotline: 1-800-787-3224

   En español: https://espanol.thehotline.org

Resources by State: https://www.womenshealth.gov/relationships-and-safety
/get-help/state-resources

Office on Women's Health: https://www.womenshealth.gov/mental-health
/get-help-now

National Indigenous Women's Resource Center: https://www.niwrc.org/resources

United Kingdom

Refuge: https://www.refuge.org.uk/get-help-now

Survivors' Network: https://survivorsnetwork.org.uk/resources

The Survivors Trust: https://www.thesurvivorstrust.org

SupportLine: https://www.supportline.org.uk/problems/rape-and-sexual-assault

Women & Girls Network: https://www.wgn.org.uk

Canada

Family Violence Resources: https://www.canada.ca/en/public-health/services/health-promotion/stop-family-violence/services.html

CASW ACTS: https://www.casw-acts.ca/en/resources/domestic-violence-resources

Ending Violence: https://endingviolencecanada.org/getting-help/

Australia

Australian Institute of Family Studies: https://aifs.gov.au/cfca/topics/web-resources-family-violence

Domestic Violence Resource Center Victoria: https://www.dvrcv.org.au/talk-someone/australia-wide-services

ReachOut: https://au.reachout.com/articles/domestic-violence-support

Respect: https://www.respect.gov.au/services

Resources for Child Abuse and Neglect

United States of America

All4Kids: https://www.all4kids.org/tools-and-resources/

Childhelp: https://www.childhelp.org/story-resource-center/child-abuse-education-prevention-resources

CDC Child Abuse and Neglect Resources: https://www.cdc.gov/violence prevention/childabuseandneglect/resources.html

United Kingdom

Support Line: https://www.supportline.org.uk/problems/child-abuse

Early Help: https://www.earlyhelppartnership.org.uk/tools-resources-charities -information-local-services-projects/Resources.aspx

NAPAC: https://napac.org.uk/about

Canada

Protect Children: https://www.protectchildren.ca/en/resources-research/survivors

Child Development Institute: https://www.childdevelop.ca/programs/family -violence-services/child-and-adolescent-services-abuse-and-trauma-casat

Australia

Raising Children: https://raisingchildren.net.au/grown-ups/services-support /services-families/child-health-services

Child Safe Organizations: https://childsafe.humanrights.gov.au/tools-resources /links-resources

Resources for First Responders, Police Officers, and Emergency Workers

United States of America

First Responder Support Network: https://www.frsn.org

Solutions for People in the Workplace: http://www.solutions-eap.com /For_Employees/Help_for_Police_Officers

United Kingdom

Blue Light Programme: https://www.mind.org.uk/news-campaigns/campaigns /blue-light-programme

Mental Health At Work: https://www.mentalhealthatwork.org.uk/toolkit /ourfrontline-emergency

Canada

First Responders First: http://www.firstrespondersfirst.ca

Boots on the Ground: https://www.bootsontheground.ca/resources

The Lifeline Canada: https://thelifelinecanada.ca/suicide-prevention-resources /first-responders

Australia

Black Dog Institute: https://www.blackdoginstitute.org.au/bush-fire-support -service/resource/emergency-service-workers

HeadsUp: https://www.headsup.org.au/healthy-workplaces/for-police-and -emergency-services

LGBTQ+ Resources

United States of America

GLAAD Resources: https://www.glaad.org/resourcelist

The Trevor Project: https://www.thetrevorproject.org

    TrevorLifeline: 1-866-488-7386, open 24 hours

    TrevorChat: https://www.thetrevorproject.org/get-help-now, open 24 hours

    TrevorText: Text START to 678-678

Trans Lifeline: 1-877-565-8860; https://www.translifeline.org

LGBTQ Psychotherapists of Color: https://www.lgbtqpsychotherapistsofcolor.com

National Queer and Trans Therapists of Color: https://nqttcn.com/en

United Kingdom

The Be You Project: https://thebeyouproject.co.uk/resources

MindOut LGBTQ Mental Health Services: https://mindout.org.uk

Switchboard: https://switchboard.lgbt/about-us

Prince's Trust: https://www.princes-trust.org.uk/help-for-young-people/who-else/housing-health-wellbeing/wellbeing/sexuality

Canada

HereToHelp: https://www.heretohelp.bc.ca/visions/lgbt-vol6/lgbt-resources

Trans Lifeline: 1-877-330-6366; https://www.translifeline.org

LGBTQ2+ Youth Line (https://www.youthline.ca): 1-800-268-9688 /
In the Toronto Area: 416.962.9688

    Telephone, text, and chat services open from Sunday to Friday, 4 p.m. to 9:30 p.m.

Australia

QLife: 1800 184 527; Webchat available at https://qlife.org.au, open every day 3 p.m.to midnight

Rainbow Network: https://www.rainbownetwork.com.au/resources

ReachOut Australia: https://au.reachout.com/articles/lgbtqi-support-services

Resources for Immigrants and Refugees

United States of America

Office for Refugee Resettlement: https://www.acf.hhs.gov/orr/resources

Immigrant Legal Resource Center (IRLC): https://www.ilrc.org /community-resources

HIAS: https://www.hias.org/who/resources-refugees

Resources for Supporting Immigrant and Refugee Communities: https://www.onlinemswprograms.com/resources/social-issues/support-resources -immigrants-refugees

Office for Victims of Crime, Human Trafficking Task Force: https://www.ovcttac.gov/taskforceguide/eguide/4-supporting-victims/44 -comprehensive-victim-services/mental-health-needs

The National Child Traumatic Stress Network: https://www.nctsn.org/resources

United Kingdom

Refugee Council: https://www.refugeecouncil.org.uk/get-support/services

Canada

Canadian Council for Refugees: https://ccrweb.ca/en/outreach-toolkit/resources

Australia

Refugee Council of Australia: https://www.refugeecouncil.org.au/resources

Finding a Therapist: Mental Health And Trauma Treatment (For Adults and Children)

Mental Health Resources for People of Color: https://www.onlinemswprograms .com/resources/social-issues/mental-health-resources-racial-ethnic-groups

Inclusive Therapists: https://www.inclusivetherapists.com

LGBTQ Psychotherapists of Color: https://www.lgbtqpsychotherapistsofcolor.com

BEAM (Black Emotional and Mental Health) Collective: https://www.beam .community

Sista Afya: https://www.sistaafya.com/resources-information

Brief Eclectic Psychotherapy (BEP): https://www.apa.org/ptsd-guideline /treatments/brief-eclectic-psychotherapy

Cognitive Behavioral Therapy (CBT): https://www.psychologytoday.com/us /therapists/cognitive-behavioral-cbt

Dialectical Behavioral Therapy (DBT): https://www.psychologytoday.com/us /therapists/dialectical-dbt

Eye Movement Desensitization and Reprocessing (EMDR): https://www.emdr .com/SEARCH/index.php

Narrative Exposure Therapy (NET): https://www.vivo.org/wp-content/uploads /2015/09/Narrative_Exposure_Therapy.pdf; https://www.frontiersin.org/articles/10 .3389/fpsyt.2020.00019/full

New England Society for the Treatment of Trauma and Dissociation: https://www.nesttd-online.org/Find-A-Therapist

Psychodynamic Therapy: https://www.psychologytoday.com/us/therapists/psychodynamic

Psychoanalytic Therapy: https://apsa.org/content/psychoanalytic-psychotherapy

Psychology Today Therapist Listing: https://www.psychologytoday.com/us/therapists

References

Alcoholics anonymous big book (4th ed.). (2002). Alcoholics Anonymous World Services.

Allen, J., Fonagy, P., & Bateman, A. (2008). *Mentalizing in clinical practice.* Washington, DC: American Psychiatric Press.

American Psychological Association. (2017). *Clinical practice guideline for the treatment of posttraumatic disorder in adults.* Retrieved October 31, 2020 from https://www.apa.org /ptsd-guideline

American Psychological Association (n.d.). Emotion regulation. In APA dictionary of psychology. Retrieved on October 31, 2020 from https://dictionary.apa.org/emotion -regulation

Benight, C. C., & Bandura, A. (2004). Social cognitive theory of posttraumatic recovery: The role of perceived self-efficacy. *Behaviour Research and Therapy, 42*(10), 1129–1148.

Bhalla, I. P., Stefanovics, E. A., & Rosenheck, R. A. (2018). Polysubstance use among veterans in intensive PTSD programs: Association with symptoms and outcomes following treatment. *Journal of Dual Diagnosis, 15,* 36. https://doi.org/10.1080/15504263 .2018.1535150

Blanchard, M. & Farber, B. A. (2016). Lying in psychotherapy: Why and what clients don't tell their therapist about therapy and their relationship. *Counselling Psychology Quarterly, 29*(1), 90–112. https://doi.org/10.1080/09515070.2015.1085365

Blanco, C., Xu, Y., Brady, K., Pérez-Fuentesa, G., Okudaa, M., & Wang, S. (2013). Comorbidity of posttraumatic stress disorder with alcohol dependence among US adults: Results from National Epidemiological Survey on alcohol and related conditions. *Drug and Alcohol Dependence 132,* 630–638.

Breslau, N., Chilcoat, H. D., Kessler, R. C., & Davis, G. C. (1999). Previous exposure to trauma and PTSD effects of subsequent trauma: Results from the Detroit area survey of trauma. *American Journal of Psychiatry 156,* 902–907.

Brewin, C. R. (2019). Complex post-traumatic stress disorder: A new diagnosis in ICD-11. *BJPsych Advances, 26*(3), 45–152. https://doi.org/10.1192/bja.2019.48

Bryan, C. J. (2019). *Crisis response planning for suicide prevention* [Power point slides]. National Center for Veterans Studies. https://avapl.org/conference/pubs/2018%20 Conference%20Presentations/Craig%20Bryan%20VA%20Leadership%20CRP.pdf.

Carrico, A. W., Gifford, E. V., & Moos, R. H. (2007). Spirituality/religiosity promotes acceptance-based responding and 12-step involvement. *Drug and Alcohol Dependence* 89(1), 66–73.

Carrico, A., Carrico, A. W., Flentje, A., Gruber, V. A., Woods, W. J., Discepola, M. V., et al. (2014). Community-based harm reduction substance abuse treatment with methamphetamine-using men who have sex with men. *UCSF*. Retrieved on October 31, 2020 from https://escholarship.org/uc/item/3r04g63v

Cloitre, M., Shevlin, M., Brewin, C. R., Bisson, J. I., Roberts, N. P., Maercker, A., Karatzias, T., Hyland, P. (2018). The International Trauma Questionnaire: development of a self-report measure of ICD-11 PTSD and complex PTSD. *Acta Psychiatrica Scandinavica, 138*(6), 536–546. https://doi.org/10.1111/acps.12956

Coates, S. W., Rosenthal, J. L., & Schechter, D. S. (2003). *September 11th: Trauma and human bonds.* Hillsdale, NJ: The Analytic Press.

Coffey, S. F., Saladin, M., Drobes, D. J., Brady, K. T., Dansky, B. S., & Kilpatrick, D. G. (2002). Trauma and substance cue reactivity in individuals with comorbid posttraumatic stress disorder and cocaine or alcohol dependence. *Drug and Alcohol Dependence, 65*(2), 115–127.

Courtwright, D., Joseph, H., & Des Jarlais, D. C. (1989). *Addicts who survived: An oral history of narcotic use in America, 1923–1965.* Knoxville, TN: University of Tennessee Press.

Courtois, C., & Ford, J. (2013). *Treating Complex Trauma: A Sequenced Relationship Based Approach.* New York, Guilford.

Crosby, A. E., Han, B., Ortega, L. A. G., Parks, S. E., & Gfroerer, J. (2011). Suicidal thoughts and behaviors among adults aged ≥18 years—United States, 2008-2009. Centers for Disease Control and Prevention, *Surveillance Summaries, 60*(SS13), 1–22.

Cukor, J., et al. (2010). Evidence-based treatments for PTSD, new directions, and special challenges. *Annals of the New York Academy of Sciences, 1208*, 82–89.

D'Anci, K. E., Uhl, S., Giradi, G., & Martin, C. (2019). Treatments for the prevention and management of suicide: A systematic review. *Annals of Internal Medicine, 171*, 334–342.

de Jongh, A., Bicanic, I., Matthijssen, S., Amann, B. L., Hofmann, A., Farrell, D., Lee, C. W., & Maxfield, L. (2019). The current status of EMDR therapy involving the treatment of complex posttraumatic stress disorder. *Journal of EMDR Practice and Research, 13*(4), 284–290. https://doi.org/10.1891/1933-3196.13.4.284

Des Jarlais, D. C. (2017). Harm reduction in the USA: The research perspective and an archive to David Purchase. *Harm Reduction Journal, 14,* 51. https://doi.org/10.1186/s12954-017-0178-6

Dimeff, L. A., Baer, J. S., Kivlahan, D. R., & Marlatt, G. A. (1999). *Brief Alcohol Screening and Intervention for College Students (BASICS): A harm reduction approach.* New York: The Guilford Press.

Dohrenwend, B. P., Turner, J. B., Turse, N. A., Adams, B. G., Koenen, K. C., & Marshall, R. (2006). The psychological risks of Vietnam for U.S. veterans: A revisit with new data and methods. *Science, 313*(5789), 979–982.

Dube, S. R., Anda, R. F., Felitti, V. J., Chapman, D. P., Williamson, D. F., & Giles, W. H. (2001). Childhood abuse, household dysfunction, and the risk of attempted suicide throughout the life span: Findings from the adverse childhood experiences study. *Journal of the American Medical Association, 286*(24), 3089–3096.

Ehlers, A., Hackman, A., Grey, N., Wild, J., Liness, S., Albert, I., et al. (2014). A randomized controlled trial of 7-day intensive and standard weekly cognitive therapy for PTSD and emotion-focused supportive therapy. *The American Journal of Psychiatry, 171*(3), 294–304. https://doi.org/10.1176/appi.ajp.2013.13040552

Foa, E., Hembree, E., & Rothbaum, B. (2007). *Prolonged exposure therapy for PTSD: Emotional processing of traumatic experiences, therapist guide.* New York: Oxford University Press.

Fonagy, P., & Allison, E. (2012). What is mentalization? The concept and its foundations in developmental research. In Midgley, N. and Vrouva, I. (Eds.), *Minding the child: Mentalization-based interventions with children, young people and their families.* (pp. 11–34). Hove, UK: Routledge.

Fraga, J. & Hendel, H. J. (2020, May 13). Questions for your prospective therapist, from your own couch. *The New York Times.* https://www.nytimes.com/2020/05/13/well/mind/prospective-therapist-interview-questions-online-virus.html

Gross, James J. (2014). *Handbook of emotion regulation, 2nd ed.* New York: The Guilford Press.

Hagelquist, J. O. (2016). The Mentalization Guidebook, 1st edition. London: Routledge.

Harvard Health Publishing (2020). Understanding the stress response. Retrieved from https://www.health.harvard.edu/staying-healthy/understanding-the-stress-response

Haslam, N. (2016, August 15). The problem with describing every misfortune as 'trauma.' *Chicago Tribune.* https://www.chicagotribune.com/opinion/ct-trauma-microaggressions -trigger-warnings-20160815-story.html.

Herman, J. L. (1992). *Trauma and Recovery.* Basic Books/Hachette Book Group.

Hoge, C. W., Auchterlonie, J. L., & Milliken, C. S. (2006). Mental health problems, use of mental health services, and attrition from military service after returning from deployment to Iraq or Afghanistan. *Journal of the American Medical Association, 295*(9), 1023–1032.

Hom, M. A., Bauer, B. W., Stanley, I. H., Boffa, J. W., Stage, D. L., Capron, D. W., et al. (2020). Suicide attempt survivors' recommendations for improving mental health treatment for attempt survivors. *Psychological Services, 18*(3), 365–376. https://doi .org/10.1037/ser0000415

Jacobsen, L. K., Southwick, S. M., Kosten, T. R. (2001). Substance use disorders in patients with posttraumatic stress disorder: A review of the literature. *American Journal of Psychiatry, 158*(8), 1184–1190. https://doi.org/10.1176/appi.ajp.158.8.1184

Joiner, T. E., Jr., Van Orden, K. A., Witte, T. K., & Rudd, M. D. (2009). The interpersonal theory of suicide: Guidance for working with suicidal clients. American Psychological Association. https://doi.org/10.1037/11869-000

Karatzias, T., Murphy, P. N., Cloitre, M., Bisson, J. I., Roberts, N. P., Shevlin, M., Hyland, P., Maercker, A., Ben-Ezra, M., Coventry, P. A., Mason-Roberts, S., Bradley, A., & Hutton, P. (2019). Psychological interventions for ICD-11 complex PTSD symptoms: systematic review and meta-analysis. *Psychological Medicine, 49,* 1761–1775.

Kaskutas, L. A. (2009). Alcoholics anonymous effectiveness: Faith meets science. *Journal of Addictive Diseases, 28*(2), 145–157. https://doi.org/10.1080/10550880902772464

Kessler, R. C., Crum, R. M., Warner, L. A., Nelson, C. B., Schulenberg, J., & Anthony, J. C. (1997). Lifetime co-occurrence of DSM-III-R alcohol abuse and dependence with other psychiatric disorders in the national comorbidity survey. *Archives of General Psychiatry 54,* 313–321.

Khantzian, E. J. (1997). The self-medication hypothesis of substance use disorders: A reconsideration and recent applications. *Harvard Review of Psychiatry, 4,* 231–244.

Kownacki, R. J., & Shadish, W. R. (1999). Does alcoholics anonymous work? The results from a meta-analysis of controlled experiments. *Substance Use & Misuse, 34*(13), 1897–1916.

Kramer, M. D., Polusny, M. A., Arbisi, P. A., & Krueger, R. F. (2014). Comorbidity of PTSD and SUDs: Toward an etiologic understanding. In P. Ouimette & J. P. Read (Eds.),

Trauma and substance abuse: Causes, consequences, and treatment of comorbid disorders (pp. 575). Washington, DC: American Psychological Association.

Lambert, M. J. (2013). The efficacy and effectiveness of psychotherapy. In M. J. Lambert (Ed.), *Bergin & Garfield's handbook of psychotherapy and behavior change* (6th ed., pp. 169–218). New York: Norton.

Laska, K. M., Gurman, A. S., & Wampold, B. E. (2014). Expanding the lens of evidence-based practice in psychotherapy: A common factors perspective. *Psychotherapy, 51*(4), 467–481. https://doi.org/10.1037/a0034332

Lee, W. K., Hayashi, K., DeBeck, K., Milloy, M. J. S., Grant, C., Wood, E., & Kerr, T. (2020). Association between posttraumatic stress disorder and nonfatal drug overdose. *Psychological Trauma: Theory, Research, Practice, and Policy, 12*(4), 373–380. https://doi.org/10.1037/tra0000511

Linehan, M. (1993). *Cognitive-behavioral treatment of borderline personality disorder.* New York: The Guilford Press.

Maercker, A., Hecker, T., Augsburger, M., & Kliem, S. (2018). ICD-11 prevalence rates of posttraumatic stress disorder and complex posttraumatic stress disorder in a German nationwide sample. *Journal of Nervous and Mental Disease, 206*(4), 270–276.

Majer, J. M., Jason, L. A., Aase, D. M., Droege, J. R., & Ferrari, J. R. (2013). Categorical 12-step involvement and continuous abstinence at 2 years. *Journal of Substance Abuse Treatment, 44*(1), 46–51.

McHugh, T., Forbes, D., Bates, G., Hopwood, M., & Creamer, M. (2012). Anger in PTSD: Is there a need for a concept of PTSD-related posttraumatic anger? *Clinical Psychology Review, 32*(2), 93–104.

Menon, R. (2019). Suicide is becoming America's latest epidemic. *The Nation.*

Moyers, T. B., Houck, J., Rice, S. L., Longabaugh, R., & Miller, W. R. (2016). Therapist empathy, combined behavioural intervention, and alcohol outcomes in the COMBINE research project. *Journal of Consulting and Clinical Psychology, 84,* 221–229.

Nahum D., Alfonso C.A., Sönmez E. (2019). Common factors in psychotherapy. In Javed A., Fountoulakis K. (Eds.), *Advances in Psychiatry.* Springer, Cham. https://doi.org/10.1007/978-3-319-70554-5_29

Najavits L. M. (2015). The problem of dropout from "gold standard" PTSD therapies. *F1000prime reports, 7,* 43. https://doi.org/10.12703/P7-43

Najavits, L. M., Weiss, R. D., & Shaw, S. R. (1997). The link between substance abuse and posttraumatic stress disorder in women: A research review. *American Journal on Addictions, 6,* 273–283.

Norcross, J. C., & Lambert, M. J. (Eds.). (2019). *Psychotherapy relationships that work. Volume 1: Evidence-based therapist contributions (3rd ed.).* New York: Oxford University Press.

Norcross, J. C., & Wampold, B. E. (Eds.). (2019). *Psychotherapy relationships that work. Volume 2: Evidence-based therapist responsiveness (3rd ed.).* New York: Oxford University Press.

Panagioti, M., Angelakis, I., Tarrier, N., & Gooding, P. (2017). A prospective investigation of the impact of distinct posttraumatic (PTSD) symptom clusters on suicidal ideation. *Cognitive Therapy and Research, 41*(4), 645–653.

Pennebaker, J. W., Kiecolt-Glaser, J. K., & Glaser, R. (1988). Disclosure of traumas and immune function: Health implications for psychotherapy. *Journal of Consulting and Clinical Psychology, 56*(2), 239–245

Pietrzak, R. H., Goldstein, R. B., Southwick, S. M., & Grant, B. F. (2011). Prevalence and Axis I comorbidity of full and partial posttraumatic stress disorder in the United States: Results from Wave 2 of the National Epidemiologic Survey on Alcohol and Related Conditions. *Journal of Anxiety Disorders, 25,* 456–465.

Pinheiro, M., Mendes, D., Mendes, T., Pais, J., Cabral, T., Rocha, J. C., et al. (2016). Importance of C-PTSD symptoms and suicide attempt. *European Psychiatry, 33*(Supplement), S215.

Putnam, F. W. (1991). Dissociative phenomena. In A. Tasman & S. M. Goldfinger (Eds.), *American Psychiatric Press review of psychiatry* (Vol. 10, pp. 145–160). Washington, DC: American Psychiatric Press.

Putnam, F. W. (1992). Discussion: Are alter personalities fragments or figments? *Psychoanalytic Inquiry 12,* 95–111.

Rauch, S., & Foa, E. (2006). Emotional Processing Theory (EPT) and exposure therapy for PTSD. *Journal of Contemporary Psychotherapy, On the Cutting Edge of Modern Developments in Psychotherapy, 36*(2), 61–65. https://doi.org/10.1007/s10879-006-9008-y

Saladin, M. E., Brady, K. T., Dansky, B. S., & Kilpatrick, D. G. (1995). Understanding comorbidity between PTSD and substance use disorders: Two preliminary investigations. *Addictive Behaviors 20,* 643–655.

Shapiro, F. (2001). EMDR: Eye Movement Desensitization of Reprocessing: Basic principles, protocols and procedures (2nd ed). New York: The Guilford Press.

Stevens, D., Wilcox, H. G., MacKinnon, D. F., Mondimore, F. M., Schweizer, B., Jancic, D., et al. (2013). Post-traumatic stress disorder increases risk for suicide attempt in adults with recurrent major depression. *Depression & Anxiety, 30*(10), 940–946.

Sullivan, C., Jones, R. T., Hauenstein, N., & White, B. (2019). Development of the trauma-related anger scale. *Assessment, 26*(6), 1117–1127. https://doi.org/10.1177/1073 191117711021

Tatarsky, A., & Marlatt, G. A. (2010). State of the art in harm reduction psychotherapy: An emerging treatment for substance misuse. *Journal of Clinical Psychology, 66*(2), 117–122.

Turecki, G. (2014). Epigenetics and suicidal behavior research pathways. *American Journal of Preventative Medicine, 47*(3 Supplement 2), S144–S151.

Ullman, S. E., Filipas, H. H., Townsend, S. M., & Starzynski, L. L. (2006). Correlates of comorbid PTSD and drinking problems among sexual assault survivors. *Addictive Behaviors, 31*(1), 128–132.

Van der Kolk, B. A. (2014). *The body keeps the score: Brain, mind, and body in the healing of trauma.* New York: Penguin Books.

Wampold B. E. (2015). How important are the common factors in psychotherapy? An update. *World psychiatry: official journal of the World Psychiatric Association (WPA), 14*(3), 270–277. https://doi.org/10.1002/wps.20238

Wampold, B. E., & Imel, Z. (2015). *The great psychotherapy debate (2nd ed.).* New York: Routledge.

Wilk, J. E., Quartana, P. J., Clarke-Walper, K., Kok, B. C., & Riviere, L. A. (2015). Aggression in US soldiers post-deployment: Associations with combat exposure and PTSD and the moderating role of trait anger. *Aggressive Behavior, 41,* 556–565.

Wolf, E. J., Miller, M. W., Kilpatrick, D., Resnick, H. S., Badour, C. L., Marx, B. P., Keane, T. M., Rosen, R. C., & Friedman, M. J. (2015). ICD-11 Complex PTSD in U.S. national and veteran samples: prevalence and structural associations with PTSD. *Clinical Psychological Science, 3*(2), 215–229. https://doi.org/10.1177/2167702614545480

Woolf, S. H., & Schoomaker, H. (2019). Life expectancy and mortality rates in the United States, 1959–2017. *Journal of the American Medical Association, 322*(20), 1996–2016.

ABOUT US

Founded by psychologist Matthew McKay and Patrick Fanning, New Harbinger has published books that promote wellness in mind, body, and spirit for more than forty-five years.

Our proven-effective self-help books and pioneering workbooks help readers of all ages and backgrounds make positive lifestyle changes, improve mental health and well-being, and achieve meaningful personal growth. In addition, our spirituality books offer profound guidance for deepening awareness and cultivating healing, self-discovery, and fulfillment.

New Harbinger is proud to be an independent and employee-owned company, publishing books that reflect its core values of integrity, innovation, commitment, sustainability, compassion, and trust. Written by leaders in the field and recommended by therapists worldwide, New Harbinger books are practical, reliable, and provide real tools for real change.

 **newharbinger**publications

Tamara McClintock Greenberg, PsyD, is a clinical psychologist and renowned expert in the treatment of depression, anxiety, trauma, and more. Her work has been published in *HuffPost*, *Psych Central*, *Psychology Today*, the *San Francisco Chronicle*, and she has been featured in *Forbes*, *USA Today*, *Newsweek*, *Next Avenue* (PBS), and *The Washington Post*. She has also been interviewed by major radio stations, including KQED's *Forum*.

FROM OUR COFOUNDER—

As cofounder of New Harbinger and a clinical psychologist since 1978, I know that emotional problems are best helped with evidence-based therapies. These are the treatments derived from scientific research (randomized controlled trials) that show what works. Whether these treatments are delivered by trained clinicians or found in a self-help book, they are designed to provide you with proven strategies to overcome your problem.

Therapies that aren't evidence-based—whether offered by clinicians or in books—are much less likely to help. In fact, therapies that aren't guided by science may not help you at all. That's why this New Harbinger book is based on scientific evidence that the treatment can relieve emotional pain.

This is important: if this book isn't enough, and you need the help of a skilled therapist, use the following resources to find a clinician trained in the evidence-based protocols appropriate for your problem. And if you need more support—a community that understands what you're going through and can show you ways to cope—resources for that are provided below, as well.

Real help is available for the problems you have been struggling with. The skills you can learn from evidence-based therapies will change your life.

Matthew McKay, PhD
Cofounder, New Harbinger Publications

**If you need a therapist, the following organization
can help you find a therapist trained in cognitive behavioral therapy (CBT).**

The Association for Behavioral & Cognitive Therapies (ABCT) Find-a-Therapist service offers a list of therapists schooled in CBT techniques. Therapists listed are licensed professionals who have met the membership requirements of ABCT and who have chosen to appear in the directory.
Please visit www.abct.org and click on Find a Therapist.

**If you need a therapist, the following organization can help you
find a therapist trained in acceptance and commitment therapy (ACT).**

Association for Contextual Behavioral Science (ACBS)
please visit www.contextualscience.org and click on Find an ACT Therapist.

For additional support, please contact the following:

National Center for PTSD
visit www.ptsd.va.gov

Anxiety and Depression Association of American (ADAA)
Please visit www.adaa.org

National Suicide Prevention Lifeline
**24 hours a day
Call, text, or chat 988
or call 1-800-273-TALK (8255)
or visit www.suicidepreventionlifeline.org**

MORE BOOKS from
NEW HARBINGER PUBLICATIONS

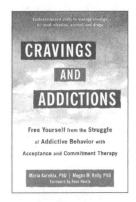
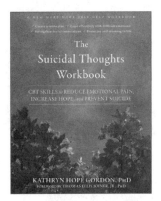
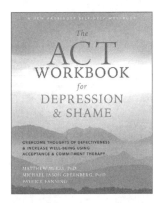

Did you know there are **free tools** you can download for this book?

Free tools are things like **worksheets**, **guided meditation exercises**, and **more** that will help you get the most out of your book.

You can download free tools for this book—whether you bought or borrowed it, in any format, from any source—from the New Harbinger website. All you need is a NewHarbinger.com account. Just use the URL provided in this book to view the free tools that are available for it. Then, click on the "download" button for the free tool you want, and follow the prompts that appear to log in to your NewHarbinger.com account and download the material.

You can also save the free tools for this book to your **Free Tools Library** so you can access them again anytime, just by logging in to your account! Just look for this button on the book's free tools page.

+ Save this to my free tools library

If you need help accessing or downloading free tools, visit **newharbinger.com/faq** or contact us at **customerservice@newharbinger.com**.